Running Shoes Are Cheaper Than Insulin: Marathon Adventures On All Seven Continents

Another Book By
Anthony "Tony" R. Reed, CPA

Other Books by Anthony Reed

the
ACHIEVEMENT
EQUATION:
YOUR
FORMULA
for
SUCCESS

by
Anthony Reed, CPA, PMP
Author of
Running Shoes Are Cheaper Than Insulin:
Marathon Adventures On All Seven Continents

WITH A NEW INTRODUCTION

Acknowledgements

I extend my thanks and appreciation to Deborah for encouraging me to pursue my dreams and for strengthening my faith.

I'd also like to thank the many friends (and their parents) whom I've met during my adventures. They include Steve, Suzie, Gillian, Jill, Donna, John, Dave, Anne, Peter, Jennifer, Phil, and others. They were kind enough to take photos of me for my journals. I'd also like to thank the many people who sent encouraging emails after reading my travel blogs.

And finally, I'd like to thank the NBMA Board of Directors, Gerald, Charlotte, Gillis, and Jacquelyn, and the members for supporting the organization.

Contact Information

Mr. Reed may be contacted for speaking engagements at

Anthony R. Reed, CPA
PO Box 180912
Dallas, TX 75218-0912
214-257-0469
Tony.Reed@AchievementEquation.com
www.AchievementEquation.com

Copyright Notice

Front cover:
Top - Humpback whale in Antarctica
Bottom – Cheetah on the Lewa Safaricom Marathon course in Kenya

Back cover: Diving penguin in Antarctica

ISBN: 978-0-9800215-2-3 (paperback)

Printed in the United States of America

First Printing – January, 2008

Published by Anthony R. Reed, CPA PC
www.AchievementEquation.com
www.Reed-CPA.com

As I crossed the finish line in my first high school cross country meet, a person said,

"You mean there are still people finishing the race?"

I finished 143rd out of 144.

This book is dedicated to those people, who

overcame the obstacles and naysayers,

stayed the course, and

finished life's races.

Table of Contents

Running Shoes Are Cheaper Than Insulin

Running Shoes Are Cheaper Than Insulin

HOW TO READ THIS BOOK

This book may be read in any sequence. I recommend reading the chapter entitled, "Running Shoes Are Cheaper Than Insulin" first. This helps to set the stage for the various trips.

The travel blogs were written during the actual trips and edited for this book. In most cases, the adventure was just getting to the destination.

While I've run almost 100 marathons, I decided to write about some of the more memorable US marathons and ultra-marathon.

PHOTOGRAPHY, CREDITS & THANKS

During my travels, I made many friends. I had to rely on their kindness, as well as complete strangers, to take photos that included me. These strangers included waiters, marathon aid station workers, other tourists, and tour guides.

I'd also especially like to thank my Texas "tour mates" for encouraging me to join them in Kenya. This allowed the three of us to complete the Seven Continents together. We had previously run marathons in China, Antarctica, and Argentina together.

The China, Antarctica, Argentina, and Africa tours were through Marathon Tours and Travel. They did an outstanding job of taking care of us.

RUNNING SHOES ARE CHEAPER THAN INSULIN

Medical Journey

When I was around seven or eight years old, I was rushed to the hospital from summer camp. I was told that I had a pre-diabetic condition and I should not have any sugar. This was a death sentence for a child who was just beginning to develop a sweet tooth.

I was told that by the time I was a teenager, I would be a diabetic and taking insulin. Every year or two, I had to take a glucose tolerance test to determine my status.

My high school years were the beginning of a major turning point. During my freshman year, students were required to participate in an organized sport during all three seasons. I ran cross-country and played soccer and baseball in the winter and spring, respectively. (My recollections of playing soccer in the cold St. Louis winters actually prepared me for the Antarctica Marathon.)

During the rest of my high school years, we were required to participate in two of the three seasons. Although I enjoyed distance running, I quit cross-country and took physical education (i.e. flag football). I continued to play soccer and switched from baseball to track and field since I couldn't hit the side of a barn.

In track, I ran in the quarter and half mile. I was mediocre. Loosely translated, I was the fifth man on a four-man relay team. I was better than the average person, but not good enough for a college track team.

Running Shoes Are Cheaper Than Insulin

During this same time period, I worked as a waiter in a small barbeque restaurant. One of the cooks had one eye. I was told that he lost his other eye to "sugar." This is what the elders called diabetes. A few years later, the cook's leg was amputated. And later, he died. Again, his death was due to the complications associated with his "sugar" or diabetes. This scared me.

I graduated from high school without taking any insulin or other prescribed medications. I felt that the active involvement in sports helped me to maintain a low body fat percentage.

In college, we were required to take a PE class. During the class, we read the books *Aerobics* and later, *New Aerobics* by Dr. Kenneth Cooper. The books stressed the importance of being physically fit as a way of improving the quality of one's life.

Dr. Cooper mentioned that some diabetics were able to decrease or completely eliminate their insulin intake. I decided to stay physically fit and "run" away from insulin. I continued running a few miles about three or four days a week.

After graduation, I moved to the Dallas/Ft. Worth, TX area. After my initial physical examination, my new doctor was surprised that I wasn't on any medications. After we talked about my running lifestyle, he said that as long as I maintain this level of fitness, I may never have to take insulin.

Later, he would let the interns conduct my physical exam and talk with them about the importance of maintaining a healthy lifestyle. He also encouraged me wear a medical ID tag. It was inscribed to state that I wasn't a diabetic and not on insulin.

During the next few years, I was running about three to five miles, five days a week. I noticed that I was spending as much time in my pre-workout and post-workout activities as I was in the workout. It took me less than 30 minutes to go running.

However, it took 30 minutes to change into my running clothes and stretch. And it took another 30 minutes to stretch, shower, and dress after the workout. I decided to consolidate my workouts to save non-workout time. So, I started running nine miles, three times a week. I saved about three hours a week.

Later, during my business career, my fitness level was the difference between getting and losing a job offer. An employer initially rescinded a job offer based on their company physical. My physician sent them a letter where he described my fitness level, including the marathons. The company extended the job offer and I was hired.

Several years later, I underwent physical exams for life insurance policies. I was initially rejected based on my body mass index (BMI). At six feet tall and 204 pounds, my BMI is around 28. This is well into the overweight range (i.e. 25 to 29.9). I was considered a risky policyholder.

However, my body fat is less than 12 percent, which puts me in the athletic or excellent category. After showing one of the medics my marathon trophy room, he included this in his report. Afterwards, I received the policy at the lower rates. On another occasion, I received the lower rates after submitting my race results and newspaper clippings.

At 52 years old, I've rarely taken any prescription medicines, including insulin. I suspect that the cost of running shoes has been a lot cheaper than insulin and high blood pressure prescriptions and higher premiums on life and medical insurance policies.

These savings helped to fund my world travel. My fitness level helped me to live a better quality of life and to get more out of the trips.

Major Influencers In My Life

As I talk with students and adults about my adventures, they inquire about the people who influenced me to achieve high goals and follow my dreams or planted the seeds for my adventures.

Here are a few of these people and how they influenced me.

Mother – Besides raising my brother and me, she introduced us to collecting stamps from around the world. She might buy a bag of one hundred stamps for a dollar. My brother and I would spend the afternoon sorting, soaking, and putting the stamps in our albums. Although we lived in the inner city, I dreamt about visiting the foreign countries where the stamps originated. It was interesting to watch the stamps change as the countries received their independence. I realized that there was more to life than my immediate neighborhood. There was an ever changing world.

Father – He taught me about patience. I learned that you have to take the time to understand a situation before you react to it. This patience was critical in holding back during the beginning of a marathon and having something for the finish. He never lost focus on the bigger picture. He continues to work out and stay fit into his eighties.

Curtiss, my brother – He taught me the spirit of adventure both domestically and internationally. During the summer of 1978, he decided to ride his bicycle about 1,200 miles from St. Louis to Vancouver, Canada. It was a solo bike ride. This was almost unheard of in 1978, especially for a 24-year-old Black man. In 1983, he went to Africa to live for most of the next eighteen years. I figured that if he could live overseas for 18 years, I could survive an 18-day tour.

Aunt Ressie – During my youth, I always heard about her international trips. She lived in Los Angeles. Although we didn't get to see her often, she would send us stamps from some of the countries. This helped to fuel my desire for traveling.

Bill – While researching my family tree, I connected with Bill over the internet. It turned out that his father and my grandfather were brothers. We were both into genealogy and computers, except that he was in his eighties.

During my trip to run Cincinnati's Flying Pig Marathon, I visited him in Dayton. As we talked about family history, he really got me thinking about my legacy. I asked myself, "What do I want people to say about me at my wake and funeral? Do I want them to say that I worked at XYZ Company for 40 years? Or do I want them to say I led a responsible, yet fun filled and exciting life?" I opted for the latter.

Bill passed away a few days before my 50th birthday celebration at the Australian Gold Coast Marathon. I think that he would have been proud of my accomplishments.

Dick – In the early 1980s, I use to see Dick running at White Rock Lake. Sometimes, we ran together. We would run nine miles at about an eight-minute pace and talk the entire time. I was shocked to learn that he was about 40 years older than me!!! He was about 65 years old. He completely changed my concept of aging and physical activity. I resolved to stay active my entire life. Dick passed away in 2007.

Deborah – After completing marathons in Antarctica and Argentina, I had planned to finish my last continent, Africa, in 2008. She taught me "to strike while the iron was hot" and to go for it. Thus, I went ahead and completed the Kenyan marathon in June, 2007.

In the process, I became the first Black in the world to complete marathons on all seven continents. She also encouraged me to rely more on my gut instincts and to trust in God through the good and challenging times. She completed her first triathlon at age 52.

Unknown St. Louis Runner – I met a fellow runner while training in Dallas one summer. He was from my hometown, St. Louis, and was visiting his son. As a Cardinal baseball fan, I asked him about the team.

He said that he use to be a big baseball fan. It wasn't unusual for him spend hours watching the games in person and on television. Then, he had triple bypass heart surgery.

He decided to stop being a couch potato and start exercising. Now, he can outrun his adult son. He told me that whenever he wanted to see an athlete, he just looked in the mirror.

Why watch an athlete or hero on television when you could be one?

Enough said...

Why Run A Marathon On Every Continent?

The two most asked questions include:

1. Why do you run marathons?
2. Why do you want to run one on every continent, especially Antarctica?

I run marathons for my health and personal enjoyment. I had initially set three lifetime goals. The first goal was to run 100 miles a month. While this seems like a lot of miles, it's only about 3 miles a day. This translates to about 30 to 40 minutes a day. I reasoned that I could sacrifice watching a television program for the sake of my health.

The second goal was to run two Texas marathons a year. My finishing times were unimportant.

These three goals forced me to stay in shape year round. As my friends became aware of these goals, they unknowingly continuously reminded me of them and held me accountable for completing them. All they did was ask me, "Are you running White Rock or Cowtown Marathon this year?" Or, "Are doing your annual birthday run this year?"

The Texas marathons were the Dallas White Rock Marathon in December and Ft. Worth's Cowtown Marathon in February. I started my White Rock training around August. The training kept me in physical shape during the summer and fall.

My Cowtown training kept me in shape during the winter. I would piggyback off of my White Rock training program. Since most weight gain occurs during the winter, I thought that this would keep me reasonably fit throughout this season.

Running Shoes Are Cheaper Than Insulin

The third goal was to run 18 miles around my birthday on July 2. This gave me a reason to continue running through the spring and early summer. Again, my finishing time was unimportant. The goal was simply to finish. Since it can easily get to over 100 degrees in the Dallas, TX summer, this was not an easy feat.

Like a lot of people, I also enjoy traveling, photography, and writing. The Seven Continents goal let me combine all of my pleasures. This goal forced me to visit places, such as Antarctica, that moved me outside of my comfort zone.

The only difference between a marathon-oriented tour and a regular tour is that I use one day to run a marathon. Most marathon courses are designed to show off the city's attractions. We usually run past the tourist spots and see the "off the beaten path" sites during the 26.2-mile runs. Since we go a slower pace than a tour bus, we're able to see more detail and interact with the people along the way.

During my first trip to Las Vegas, I awoke very early in the morning and went for a short run. I located all of the casinos, places to eat, and other attractions and became very familiar with the city. Now, when I visit a city, I go for a run.

Shadowboxing & Quilts

My tax client's husband was a professional baseball player. The first time I walked into their home, my eyes were immediately drawn to a large shadowbox. It held his Oakland A's World Series jersey.

I dreamt that I could achieve something that was so spectacular that it would warrant putting a running jersey inside a shadow box. After completing Australia's Gold Coast Marathon on my 50th birthday, I decided to make a one to commemorate the event.

After it was complete, I decided to make one using the running jersey from each of my international marathons. As luck would have it, I still had the t-shirt that I wore in my first marathon, 23 years earlier, and my European marathon!!!

Running Shoes Are Cheaper Than Insulin

Each shadowbox contains, at a minimum, the

- running jersey or t-shirt that was worn
- currency from the country
- country's flag
- race number
- race photo
- souvenirs, such as boomerangs (Australia) and tour tickets (China)
- trinkets, such as 50th birthday cards (Australia), tour luggage tags (China), a coin to use the restroom (Denmark), whistle (Antarctica) & plastic hotel keys (Argentina)

After my 50th birthday, I found myself with about 60 marathon t-shirts hanging in my overcrowded closet. I had a quilt made from 24 of them. The remaining t-shirts were given to a homeless shelter.

Since I had run some of the marathons multiple times, I selected my favorite from each series. The quilt also includes the t-shirts from completing a 100-mile bike rally and the Texas Marathon Challenge.

The t-shirts are separated by black vertical and horizontal borders. The horizontal borders were embroidered with the significant athletic endurance achievements as of my 50th birthday. This included completing

- 68 Marathons
- 15 States
- 3 Continents
- 1 Bike Century

I decided to make the quilt a "living" trophy. Whenever I finished a marathon in a different State, I put a lapel pin, which was in the shape of the State, on the vertical border in the quilt's center. If I completed multiple marathons in the same State, I included a State flag. When I completed an international marathon, a country flag pin is added to the center horizontal border. Also, if I went for a training run in a foreign city, I added a city pin, such as the Eiffel Tower.

What's Next?

While on the tour in China, we had a discussion about our next goal upon completing the seventh continent. For most of us, China was our fourth continent. As I moved closer to completing my goal, the "What's next?" question became more prevalent amongst runners and non-runners alike.

It occurred to me that once you start achieving goals, other people expect and, in some cases, almost demand that you set higher or more interesting goals. Your life becomes the discussion topic at the office water cooler and parties. People start living vicariously through your adventures and achievements. Thus, they want to know "What's next?"

During this journey, I found myself meeting high achievers in other areas, most notably Mt. Everest climbers. I've always wanted to see Mt. Everest and at least visit the first level base camp. One thing that I've learned from my travels is that actually being at a location and experiencing it is much more exciting than looking at a photo or video. Some friends found a Mt. Everest Marathon.

On the other hand, we also discussed running races on all seven continents—again. However, this time it would be on islands. The locations may include:

North America	Jamaica
South America	Easter Island
Africa	Madagascar
Europe	London
Oceania	New Zealand
Asia	Japan
Antarctica	King George Island

So, for now, I haven't decided what's next. However, it will be fun.

THE ACHIEVEMENT EQUATION BOOK EXCERPT

I spent many successful years as an information technology executive. In the process, I saved companies millions of dollars on projects by combining project management and distance running techniques. This process was described in my 2007 book, The Achievement Equation – Your Formula For Success. An excerpt from the introduction follows.

Achievement

Noun: something accomplished, especially by superior ability, *special effort*, great courage, etc.

Synonyms: Achievement connotes final accomplishment of something noteworthy, after much effort and often *in spite of obstacles and discouragements.*

Source: *Dictionary.com*

Over the years, the Achievement Equation has evolved into a powerful tool to meet, if not exceed, your personal and professional goals. The Achievement Equation draws you into the nexus where business strategies and endurance running strategies overlap.

Running Shoes Are Cheaper Than Insulin

Our process brings into focus those points where project management skills converge with distance running techniques to produce outstanding results. The business strategies include project, change, and time techniques. The running techniques include stress and risk management, pacing, and goal setting.

The Achievement Equation draws from the combined experience of high-achieving individuals from around the world. It makes no difference whether the individual manages a quarter billion dollar portfolio or the complicated social dynamics of a small African village— each draws from compatible, if not identical, equations for success.

Successful high school and college students, refugee camp managers, professional athletes, runners, bicyclists, ministers, traditional leaders, educators, mountain climbers, and business people, among others, rely on the same variables in the Achievement Equation.

Despite our varied backgrounds, we shared a common characteristic: our ability to overcome failure and obstacles. People are impressed with my academic background; two undergraduate degrees (mathematics and management), an MBA (management), and an MS (accounting). I was also a member of the Accounting Honor Society. However, in my junior year in college I received a letter, which read, in part:

"After reviewing your academic records for the past and previous semesters, I have decided that you should be placed on Academic Suspension status."

The letter was from the university's Assistant Dean. I was suspended for poor grades. Not only did I lose my scholarship, but also my residential advisor position in the dorms.

In order for me to achieve the goal of obtaining a college degree, I had to overcome a major obstacle—me.

When I overcame that self-imposing obstacle, my academic performance improved. In time, I earned an undergraduate degree in mathematics and another in management, as well as a masters of business administration, and a masters of science in accounting.

THE ACHIEVEMENT EQUATION COMPONENTS

A job recruiter contacted my three job references to discuss my qualifications for an executive position. Near the end of each phone call, he asked them the same open-ended question, "In three words or less, how would you best describe Tony?" Much to his surprise, they used the same phrase: "goal-oriented."

He then asked them to give one or two specific instances that supported their description. They each gave accounts of situations in completely different areas to support their description. One person focused on my literary, academic, and professional certification achievements. Another emphasized my athletic accomplishments. And the third stressed my professional project management completions.

The recruiter was so impressed that he encouraged me to write a book. Subsequently, I wrote my first book: The SMART Degree – A Young Professional's Guide To Reality. SMART was an acronym for systems, management, accounting, and related technologies. This led to national speaking engagements about multi-disciplinary goal setting.

Running Shoes Are Cheaper Than Insulin

Over the next few years, I followed up with some of the people who attended my presentations. I found that their lives had not changed very much. They set goals, but didn't know how to implement them. This led to frustration and abandonment of their dreams.

As I re-examined my personal life and talked with other achievers, it became obvious that goal setting was just one of four components that are necessary to reach our objectives. The other components are motivation, planning, and execution. Failure to follow through on any one of these components leads to a failure to achieve the goals.

Failure to set goals leads to a life without direction. This person is aimless. He may be well motivated, but without a goal (or direction), he's like a dog chasing his tail. There's a lot of activity, but it's spent running around in circles. And when you're finished, you're standing right where you started.

A lack of motivation means that even the most well-defined goal may never be achieved. The individual is too lazy to execute their plan. Or they may start and stop only to never finish. Think about the number of people who say that they want a diploma or degree, but fail to graduate from high school or college.

Once a goal is properly defined and the person is well motivated, they must develop a plan. Without a plan, a person wastes precious energy and resources. The resources include money, other people's time and energy, and materials. Once people see that you're wasting resources, they may not want to help you.

Also, good planning forces you to face the risks associated with reaching your goals. These risks represent your weaknesses. If you don't acknowledge and mitigate your risks/weaknesses before you execute your plan, you may find yourself making the wrong decisions under stressful situations and wasting resources to combat the problem. You must face your weaknesses to succeed.

And last, but not least, failure to execute the plan means that the goal will not be achieved. Many well-thought-out plans have been left on the floor because people weren't motivated to execute the individual tasks. It's ironic that *execute* is not only defined as a positive action (i.e. to a perform), but also as a negative action (i.e. to kill). This final component ultimately "makes or breaks" the Achievement Equation.

These four components (i.e. goal setting, motivation, planning, and execution) work together to form the Achievement Equation.

After I realized the relationship between the components, I found myself accepting and completing more challenging assignments as a business executive. Our vice president of finance called me into his office to discuss a proposal for a global information technology project. We needed to upgrade all the business' mission critical Oracle applications. These included the financial, order management, supply chain, logistics, sales, and web store applications.

He estimated the project would cost between $10 to $12 million. His estimate was based on his research of previous upgrades and the original cost to implement the applications. He wanted me put together a proposal and budget for the project.

A couple of weeks later, I returned with a high-level project plan and a proposed budget. I had estimated that the project would cost about $4 million. This was substantially less than his estimate. Needless to say, there was a lot of reservation on his part that the plan would succeed.

About a year later, we discovered that my estimate was incorrect. The project was completed at a cost of $2.6 million!!! It was on time, under budget, and to specifications.

The Achievement Equation – Your Formula For Success may be purchased at the web store at:

www.Reed-CPA.com.

NORTH AMERICA (USA) - COWTOWN MARATHON

Date: February 27, 1982
Marathon Number: 1International Marathon Number: 1
Inspirational Song: "Ain't No Stoppin Us Now"
performed by McFadden & Whitehead

Running Shoes Are Cheaper Than Insulin

Race Selection Process

In February 24, 1979, I was a graduate student at Texas Christian University in Ft. Worth, TX. An ice storm had hit the city and many businesses had closed. I decided to continue with my Saturday ritual of studying in the library. As I approached University Blvd., I noticed runners wearing race numbers. It was cold, icy, and slippery. I thought that they were crazy. That night, the news reported that they had held the first Cowtown Marathon.

A couple of years later, I was a part of our corporate 10K team at the Cowtown Marathon. A friend and I were waiting for our race to begin when we heard a gunshot. We thought that it was our race. We ran to the starting line only to be told that it was for the marathon.

As I saw the runners' physiques, I realized that all marathoners weren't short, pencil-thin runners. Some of them looked like me: six-feet tall and 180 pounds. A few months later, David and I decided to train for the 1982 Cowtown Marathon.

Race Day

In preparing for the marathon, we read books and any magazines that we could find. We were told that you shouldn't enter a marathon unless you could finish it in less than four hours. Unfortunately, there weren't marathon training groups. We were reduced to talking with experienced runners, reading, and mostly "trial and error."

The magazines included "The Runner", "Running Through Texas", "Runner's World." I had previously experimented with carrying and drinking water, soft drinks (including de-fizzed and diluted), and juices, including grapefruit juice. I still have a magazine page from "Running Through Texas" with the recipe for making your own electrolyte in the November, 1983 edition. (The back of the page has an entry form for the 1984 Cowtown Marathon. It cost $10 for either the 10K or marathon. The late entry fee was $15.)

Our reference books are considered classics and I still use them. They included:

- Dr. Sheehan on Running by George Sheehan, MD
- The Runner's Handbook by Bob Glover and Jack Shepherd
- The Complete Runner by the editors of Runner's World Magazine
- The Complete Book of Running by James F. Fixx
- The Complete Marathoners edited by Joe Henderson
- Marathoning: A Book by Manfred Steffny

It was cold when the Cowtown Marathon started. Since running tights hadn't been invented, we either wore sweat pants or women's pantyhose to keep warm. I overdressed and found myself throwing off sweat clothes after the first three miles.

The toughest part of the course was at the Hulen Street Bridge around 17 miles. As I ran towards the bridge, I saw runners stop and turn into the crowd. I thought that we made a right turn and didn't have to climb the hill.

Much to my surprise, those runners were quitting the race!!! I decided to continue running and not quit. The hill was brutal. (Several years later, they changed the course. Marathoners run down the hill at the early part of the race.)

Cowtown had one the best final 0.2-mile finish lines. I recall turning the corner at 26 miles, hearing the crowd, and seeing a steep downhill stretch. It was almost impossible to walk down the hill without running. This made even the most tired runner pick up his pace for the crowd.

The clock flashed 3:57. My goal was a sub-four hour marathon. I had to really "haul it" to make my goal. A fellow runner and I sprinted to the finish line. As we crossed it, they yelled out my time, gave me a trophy, and handed me a small piece of paper. It was stamped with my overall place. I had to fill in my race number, name, age, sex, and finishing time. There's nothing like trying to write legibly in small spaces after running 26.2 miles. (Finishing time technology has come a long way.) I met my goal. My official time was 3:59:23.

Post-Race Comments

Several months later, I learned that Cowtown was the toughest course in Texas. I had actually survived the marathon and met my goal. Between 1982 and 2007, I have returned to this marathon seventeen times. I returned to run my 50th Texas marathon in 2004. My fastest time on this course was 3:41:46.

Lessons Learned

- Sometimes, you must visually see an event as a spectator before you actually do it. So, I'll expose my children to many different events.
- You never know what the residual benefits of reaching a goal will be.
- At the beginning of a marathon, dress as though the temperature will be twenty degrees higher than it will be when you anticipate finishing the race, instead of dressing for according to the temperature at the beginning of the race.

- Despite my physique, I can run marathons.

EUROPE (DENMARK) - TAILWINDS MARATHON

Date: July 25, 2004
Marathon Number: 58
International Marathon Number: 2
Inspirational Song: "We're A Winner" performed by
The Impressions (with Curtis Mayfield)

Race Selection Process

Prior to starting my international marathon adventures, my three international travel experiences consisted of a bus ride to Montreal, Canada in 1969, a five-day vacation in Ochs Rios, Jamaica, and walking across the US/Mexico border bridge for an evening in Tijuana.

I was the sole supporter for my family; a wife and two children. I had postponed my international marathon adventures until either the children were out of high school, my wife obtained employment, or my company sent me out of the country.

As luck would have it, I was going to be sent to Europe for a series of meetings in Germany, Belgium, and The Netherlands. Upon hearing the news, I immediately began to search for a European marathon to run during my free weekend. I became very good "friends" with the website called MarathonGuide.com. I had to decide between Germany, Sweden, Switzerland, Norway, and Denmark marathons.

It was a complete "crap shoot." I didn't speak any of these languages and didn't have any contacts in the countries. I began to eliminate the marathons systematically. Some didn't have English versions of their websites. Other's had very challenging courses. I visualized myself being lost in the snow-covered mountains or in the forest and they didn't find my body until a year later. I also looked at the plane schedules and the ease of getting to and from the race using public transportation.

By process of elimination, I selected the Medvinds (Tailwinds) Marathon in Copenhagen, Denmark. It started in Copenhagen and went north along the shoreline to Helsinger.

Running Shoes Are Cheaper Than Insulin

According to the website, "The Tailwind marathon is arranged by runners for runners as a back-to-basic marathon race without grand prizes etc.—which is reflected in the start fee, which is 150 Danish kroner (DKK), 20 US dollars or 25 euro." The race was so low key that there would not be any:

- Printed material - Everything would be handled via the website.
- Race numbers.
- Manned aid stations – You brought your own electrolytes.
- Medical aid stations or assistance.
- Finisher medals.
- Portable toilets – You had to use the toilets in the train depots. This assumes that you know their location along the course.
- Closed off streets – The traffic would be moving at its regular pace.
- Street crossing guards – You had to watch out for cars and obey the traffic signals.
- Sag wagon – The directions for quitting were also posted on the website. "If you drop out of the race, you can take the "Kystbanetog" (train) towards Elsinore Station (every 20th minute) or bus 388 from "Strandvejen" to the finishing line. We recommend that you carry a yellow card (non-used ticket for multiple destinations) during the race. The yellow card can be bought at train stations or in buses within 30 kilometres from Copenhagen. Please inform the staff at the nearest depot if you're dropping out."

The website summed up the demands on the participants by stating, "Basically, participation is on your own responsibility—Pay attention to your body and the surrounding world." Needless to say, this wasn't anything like the mega-marathons in the US.

Since there was a time limit for finishing the marathon, we had to submit our fastest times for either the half marathon or the full marathon in the previous twelve months for review. The results were subsequently posted on the race's website.

Much to my surprise, I would finish dead last by about 30 minutes!!! I estimated that after the first twenty minutes of the race, I would lose sight of the runners and be on my own. I was also the only American out of the 58 runners.

Therefore, for the first time in my life, I had to prepare to finish in last place in a marathon without any assistance in a foreign country where I didn't speak the language. This was going to be an adventure.

Pre-Race Day Activities

I decided to scout out the starting area the day before the marathon. This allowed me to learn the bus and train schedules and note any special considerations. With my trusty map and high spirits, I departed the hotel for the walk to the bus stop.

Fortunately, I had to take the bus from my hotel back to the airport. Naturally, I thought that the bus stop would be across the street from the same stop they dropped me off on Friday. After waiting for a period of time, someone from the hotel came out and explained that the bus had a different weekend schedule. Much to my surprise, the correct bus stop was actually three blocks away. I quickly visualized myself waiting for the race-day bus that never arrived.

Running Shoes Are Cheaper Than Insulin

I had no problems transferring from the bus to the train at the airport. Finding the right depot was also not a problem. However, the real adventures began after leaving the train. According to the race instructions, the closest public toilet to the starting line was the depot.

Much to my surprise, you had to pay to use the commode and there wasn't a change machine around. Furthermore, the depot was about one-third of a mile away from the starting line!!! Thus, there was no option to go to the restroom a few minutes before the marathon started.

Although I was Boy Scout and prided myself on my sense of direction, I was completely lost after departing the depot. There was some street construction at the depot. The detours threw off my sense of direction. When I finally located the starting line area, I felt comfortable and confident that I could find it on race day. This relieved a great deal of race-day pressure.

I managed to make my way back to the hotel without any problems. My dinner consisted of a Domino's pizza. This tasted just like home and was added to my post-race meal list. Based on previous race-day disasters, I set the alarms on my watch, cell phone, PDA, and hotel room radio. I also left a wakeup call message for the front desk.

On the eve of a previous marathon, we lost the power in our house. I awoke 45 minutes before the race to see my clock blinking midnight. As result of this experience, I don't rely 100 percent on electrical alarms that plug into wall outlets.

The rest of the evening was spent laying out and packing all of my race-day clothes and items. As the last place finisher in a foreign country, I realized that I needed to carry special items with me during the race. These included:

- My passport
- Copy of my medical record
- Change for toilets
- Change for transportation
- 100 Euros for medical emergencies
- Electrolyte fluids
- Map
- Credit Card(s)

Since I knew that once I left the hotel I would not return for 12 hours, I made a list of everything that I needed to take with me. If an item wasn't important, it wasn't on the list. Thus, items as simple as sunglasses were on the list.

Race Day Activities

The morning was prefect as I left the hotel around 7AM. It was overcast and cool. The bus and train rides went very well. I took care of my personal business in the depot's restroom and walked to the starting line. Much to my surprise, there was only one other person at the starting line 45 minutes before the start. People finally started arriving about 15 minutes later.

Boxes were set out for us to put in our bottles of water or electrolytes. The boxes were labeled in 5K increments from 5K through 35K. Since there were no manned aid stations, you placed your fluids in the appropriate box and they were dropped off on tables along the route. I placed my clearly identifiable bottles in the 15K (9.3-mile) and 30K (18.6-mile) boxes.

Fortunately, as luck would have it, the race director had enough paid entrants to afford race numbers.

Running Shoes Are Cheaper Than Insulin

As soon as the race started, so did the rain. It continued to rain throughout the day. After 3K, I was running alone. After 5K, I didn't see the runners in front of me. Fortunately, we had kilometer signs along the course. Thus, the only way I could tell if I was still on the course was by seeing a kilometer marking every 6 to 7 minutes.

I saw only one directional sign during the entire 26.2 miles. This wasn't bad until I approached a major intersection between 11K and 12K. I spotted a directional arrow that was nailed to a lamppost. Unfortunately, it was on one nail and was spinning around like a windmill.

I didn't even know if it was related to the race or another event. Since it was a point-to-point course, I knew that I wasn't supposed to turn around. Thus, I had a one in three chance of going in the right direction.

As luck would have it, I took the wrong turn. I made a right turn because I knew that the course followed the shoreline, which was on my right. Fortunately, since the race director was able to afford race numbers, a couple of motorists told me that I was off the course. Unfortunately, they didn't tell me which way to go when I returned to the "spinning arrow" intersection.

By this time, I had a 50-50 chance of picking the right direction. As luck would have it, I went the wrong way, again.

While I wasted over 20 minutes during this fiasco, I considered myself to be an explorer or adventurer. I told myself that if I could survive this low-key, no frills "runners" marathon in a foreign country in the wind and rain and communicate without knowing the language, then I could survive anything.

I was conservative regarding my fluid consumption. Since there weren't any easily accessible restrooms along the course, I wanted to avoid any pit stops. As I approached the 15K "aid table," I was relieved to see my water bottle. I decided to withhold some fluids in reserve.

At the 30K table, things went wrong. Someone had removed half of the electrolytes. I didn't know whether or not they drank from the bottle or just poured some out. I played it safe and left the bottle. I nursed my 15K to the finish line.

As I approached the finish line, I noticed my backpack with my dry clothes sitting in a puddle on the ground. My clothes were soaked. However, as I crossed the finish line, the race director, much to my surprise, handed me a finisher's medal. My time was five hours, thirty-four minutes, and twenty-eight seconds. I finished.

I was cold, wet, and starving. I walked about a mile to the metro train station (and the nearest restroom). Unfortunately, the food stand was closed. Thus, I sat in wet clothes for the one-hour return trip to the hotel by the metro train and bus. I left for the race at 7AM and returned to my room 12 hours later. After a hot shower, that Dominos pizza never tasted so good. While I finished dead last in the race, I finished in the top 50 and was the first American!!! There's always a bright side to finishing a marathon—if you look closely!!!

Post-Marathon Events

Upon returning to the US, I was excited about my adventure. Most of my co-workers were equally excited. A week after my return, my manager called me into his office. Evidently, someone "complained" that I had arranged the business trip to coincide with the marathon!!! This "complaint" was also brought to the attention of our Human Resources Vice President. She identified the complainant.

It didn't matter that the marathon was held on a Sunday, I paid all of my own expenses, and I didn't miss any office time. It didn't matter that there were about three of four marathons every weekend in Europe during the running season. It didn't even matter that I didn't select the dates for the business trip.

What mattered was that an insecure person felt threatened by a goal-oriented athlete and business professional. While the executives had to agree that the allegations were completely groundless, I was told that I shouldn't run marathons on business trips, even if it's on my own time and at my own expense.

Lessons Learned

- Prepare for the worst. Carry my own fluids and food.
- Consider every misfortune to be an adventure.
- Carry money during the race. (In other marathons, I used the money to purchase food and drinks during the races and items for sale after the races.)

OCEANIA (AUSTRALIA) - GOLD COAST MARATHON

Date: July 3, 2005 (50th Birthday)
Marathon Number: 68
International Marathon Number: 3
Inspirational Song: "My Island Home" performed by
Christine Anu

Running Shoes Are Cheaper Than Insulin

Race Selection Process

Since I ran my first marathon, I always wanted to run one on my 50th birthday—July 2, 2005. For many years, I thought that the San Francisco Marathon would be that race. It was held in early July. However, in 2002, it was moved to the last Sunday in July.

In January 2005, I began searching for my birthday marathon. I had two choices: the Leadville (CO) Trail Marathon on July 2 or the Gold Coast Marathon on July 3 in Australia. I realized that Australia is a day ahead of the US. Therefore, I could celebrate my birthday over two days: July 2 in the Australian time zone and July 2 in the Central Time Zone, which is July 3 in Australia.

For almost a year leading up to the marathon, my spouse and I were having marital problems. We were approaching the "empty nest" time period. Our youngest child had started college away from home. As a "peace offering," I thought that it would be good for my wife and me to celebrate in Australia. I even purchased a ticket for our daughter. I felt that this would show my spouse that I was fully committed to our marriage.

The Monday before we were to depart, my wife called me at work. She informed me that she was leaving to go on vacation near Houston. This was the first time that I knew about this one-week vacation. She would return in time for us to go to Australia. I couldn't understand why she would spend the money in Houston instead of saving it for Australia. None of this made sense. So, I decided to go to Australia alone.

Travel Problems

My goal of running a marathon on every continent almost
ended on this trip. I had a slight panic attack on the
departing flight. I've taken airplane trips without any
problems since the mid-seventies. I had even flown to
Europe without any problems. However, the Australian
flight represented my worst nightmare.

I had booked the flight on one airline. However, the flight
was actually with one of their partners. Unfortunately, this
meant that I could not select my seat. While most people
prefer the window seat, I prefer the aisle. At six-feet tall
and 200 pounds, I have wide shoulders and big legs. Thus,
I feel cramped in a window seat. I like to "spill over" and
put my foot into the aisle. I was given the window seat for
this 20+ hour flight, which had a nighttime departure.

As luck would have it, the flight was also packed with about
100 youths going to a People to People conference in
Sydney. Furthermore, I was sitting next to a teenage girl.
Her talkative boyfriend had the aisle seat. I felt like a
sardine in a can. As the flight departed, the pilot pointed
out the flight map on the seat's video monitor. It tracked
our altitude and estimated arrival time.

After dinner, the lights were turned off. The passenger in
front of me let his seat back. There was about one inch
between my knees and the back of their seat and about
three inches between my face and the video screen. My
right shoulder was smashed against the window. I was in a
coffin. At this moment, the girl's boyfriend was trying to
impress her. It was her first plane trip. He boldly point out
that we had 20 hours remaining before we landed!!!

I panicked. There was no way I could sit like this for over
20 hours. I felt a bead of sweat roll down my forehead and

my armpits became moist. I got up and went to the flight attendant. Unfortunately, there were no aisle seats available, except in business class. I held out my credit cards and asked to be moved to business class. Since he couldn't verify how much I paid for my seat and didn't know the business class fare, he couldn't charge me the difference. I couldn't be upgraded. I considered standing during the entire flight. I even thought about locking myself in a restroom to spread out. I was stuck.

He proceeded to give me advice on how to survive the long journey. He said for me to loosen my seat belt. He told me to visualize that I was playing a hand held or portable video game. He pointed out that people get so captivated by the activity on the small screen that they're completely unaware of their surroundings, such as small spaces like an airline seat. Since each passenger had a video console with movies and games, I could preoccupy myself with checkers or solitaire. He also suggested walking around the cabin.

He concluded his advice with an interesting observation. He said that he wasn't worried about me. He was concerned about another passenger. This Texan was about 6' 6" and weighed about 300 pounds. He had a middle seat in the coach "cattle car." My physique was nothing compared to this man's dimensions. I began to realize that he was in much worse shape than I was.

I decided to walk around for a few minutes to regain my composure. I ran into the Texan at the back of the plane's cross-over aisle. His head was pressed against his forearm while his forearm was on the wall. I startled him. We discussed our fears and came to several realizations:

- They weren't going to turn the plane around.
- They weren't going to upgrade us.

- We couldn't walk out of the plane at 35,000 feet.
- We didn't want to disturb the children.
- We couldn't stay on our feet for 20 hours.

We were stuck. We also realized that we had to fly back on the same type of airplane. I visualized myself asking my manager to have my vacation time extended while I took a ship back to the US. Or I could just find a job and stay in Australia.

After a couple of hours of talking and calming down, I returned to my seat and woke up the teenage couple. As I prepared to refocus and play video checkers, the boyfriend pointed out to his girlfriend that we only had 15 hours to go!!! I panicked and immediately excused myself again. After a couple of more hours of pacing, I returned to my seat and fell asleep. I felt sorry for the tall Texan.

Travel Log

After my European trip, I decided to keep travel logs to help me remember my adventures. Here are excerpts from this Australian adventure.

Written on the flight from DFW to LA.

This trip represents my birthday present to myself. As Marcia Ann Gillespie implied, "If you wait for other people to tell you that you've done a good job or to reward you, you'll be waiting a long time. Therefore, you should recognize your own accomplishments and reward yourself." [Note: Marcia Ann Gillespie spoke to the students at Washington University where I was an undergraduate student. She was the editor of *Essence* magazine.]

Running Shoes Are Cheaper Than Insulin

This is my reward for reaching 50 years old. Along the way, I've:

- Never being arrested
- Never smoked
- Not been on drugs
- Provided support for a family of four
- Never missed a school event for either child
- Gave both children a head start in life by teaching them to read
- Put my wife through graduate school
- Earned two undergraduate degrees
- Earned two graduate degrees
- Passed the CPA exam
- Ran 50 marathons before turning 50
- Was faithfully married for 24 years

Tony, to paraphrase the beer commercial, "This trip is for you!!!"

Written June 30 in Australia

The first two fast-food places coming out of customs were Krispy Kreme and McDonald's. I had decided to eat a Big Mac in every country I visited. I wanted to see if they taste like home. This one needed extra salt.

I finally arrived in Brisbane after the brief layover in Sydney. The customs agent was more concerned about me bringing in beef jerky (mad cow disease) than the other food in my luggage. I declared my canned fruit, packaged tuna, and M&M's. Since I'm from Texas, they even inspected my running shoes for dirt.

In Brisbane and the Gold Coast, it had rained so much that the roads leading to the Gold Coast were actually flooded. I had to take a long detour to get to the Gold Coast.

Written 5:30AM, Thursday, July 1, Gold Coast

The day that I left Dallas, I purchased a tour book on Australia. It was the first time that I noticed that the Aussies drive on the left side of the road. This was going to be weird.

I rented a Hertz Toyota Camry. It was very interesting. I actually stared at the car for about five minutes before I got in. I was debating about whether or not I should take the bus to the Gold Coast.

I knew that the steering wheel and foot pedals would be on the right side. However, the brake pedal was still on the left side and the gas was still on the right side. I thought that they would have been reversed. This made driving easier.

The main problem that I experienced was using the turn signal and windshield wiper control. They were reversed. Thus, when I wanted signal to change lanes, I turned the wipers on by mistake.

On the plane, I was reading <u>A Gathering of Old Men</u> by Ernest J. Gaines. It seems appropriate for an "old man" to read. I happened to see the movie on TV One before I left. However, the book gets more into the characters. I like the fact the old men found a cause to unite them. They realized that at some point in your life, you have to "throw caution and tradition to the wind" and take a stand for your relatives and yourself before you die.

They took that opportunity to be the men that society had prevented them from being. I also like the fact they were

Running Shoes Are Cheaper Than Insulin

doing it in front of their grandchildren. I'm sure that it's something that they themselves will remember.

Yesterday, I had a massage in my hotel room ($66 AU). It felt great after the plane ride. My right shoulder was aching from being jammed against the plane's window. My left one was stiff from carrying the luggage. The massage felt so good that I ordered another one for 2PM on race day.

This morning, I finished reading the book. In light of the recent stateside events, there was a very interesting passage in the book. It read, "Sometimes you got to hurt something to help something. Sometimes you have to plow under one thing in order for something else to grow."

I ventured out this morning for a walk. I "discovered" the ocean and stood on the beach. Next, I walked to the Paradise Centre and Cavill Mall to explore. I bought some souvenirs and birthday cards for my daughter and me. I was also looking for a CD by an Aussie artist named Christine Anu. The song was called "My Island Home." If I don't find it before I leave, I'll order it over the Internet.

I mailed Kristy her birthday card. I thought that it would be "cool" to get a card from a foreign country. I went to the race expo. My race number was 206. The Expo was very, very small and was held in a tent. I purchased a running singlet and a polo shirt with the marathon logos. These were my birthday presents to myself.

After the registration process, I went across the street and watched "War of the Worlds." I then retired back to the hotel for a dinner of tuna and crackers with chocolate milk. Since the pain returned to my shoulder (from the flight), I took a couple of painkillers.

I realized that I'd have two birthdays (or my birthday would span two days): an early one in Australia and my real one in the US. I'll run the marathon on my birth date in the US.

Written 7PM, July 2 (50th Birthday)

Happy Aussie Birthday to me!!! Tomorrow will be my US birthday. After having the hotel's breakfast buffet, I returned to the mall and purchased a back scrubber. I also decided to get another singlet. This one will be framed along with my race number and other trip stuff, such as the flag decal, boomerang, and finisher's medal.

I spent part of the morning at an outdoor crafts & discount market. It was a lot like a farmers market. Next, I explored another mall and purchased a double disc CD called "Cheezy Cuts - The Ultimate Cheese Party." It has everything from "I'm Too Sexy" to "Macarena." It's truly cheesy.

I returned to the hotel, camped out on the balcony, and watched the waves and surfers. I also began to think seriously about pursuing a Ph.D.

Although the TV/cable channels are limited, they have a channel called "Party Max." It plays some very good music videos that I don't see in the US. Also, the water goes down the drain in a counter-clock fashion. [Note: It goes clockwise in the northern hemisphere.]

It costs $2 AU for 15 minutes of Internet access. While I check my hotmail once a day, I'm very proud that I haven't looked at my work email.

It still feels a little weird driving on the left side of the road. I actually had to parallel park again. I'm getting better. However, I still turn on the wipers to change lanes.

Running Shoes Are Cheaper Than Insulin

Written Sunday, July 3 at 6:04 PM (Race Day)

I awoke at 5AM to dress for the race. At 5:45, I was at the bus stop, which was across the street from the hotel. The race started under prefect weather.

Since the racecourse was measured in kilometers, I had to convert my pace. Thus, my pace would be about 7 minutes per kilometer. I decided that when my pace dips to 7:30 for three consecutive K's, I would then "shut it down" and just finish the race. This happened around 30K (18.6 miles).

Around 32K, I ran into a runner from Dallas. What a small world!!! I crossed the finish line in 5:22. It was my 68th marathon, on my third continent, and on my 50th birthday. What a present!!!

I'm not sure that my body will take running a marathon in every state. I have 35 states to go. However, one on every continent is definitely doable. I'm thinking about running the half marathon in Antarctica, instead of the full. When I return to Dallas, I need to get the winter and spring schedules for Amberton University and look at races in South America and Asia for 2006.

After the race, I had a scrub brush shower and a well-deserved massage.

Written 4:27 PM, July 5

Yesterday morning after the marathon, I felt fine. I was excited about going on the tour of the Hinterlands. It's also known as Lamington National Park. It's a rain forest. The trip was very, very cool.

We visited the "Best of All Lookout." This was located on the lip of the crater rim. The crater is about 80K or 50 miles across. My photo was taken at this location. Unfortunately, my camera's battery door broke and I was unable to take any more photos.

On our way to the lookout point, we saw "Antarctica trees." These are the trees that remained after Australia broke off from Antarctica. It's ironic that during the Birmingham Mercedes Marathon, I ran through the "pink pig" decorated neighbor right after I was trying to select my next marathon. Subsequently, I registered for the Flying Pig Marathon. Ironically, today I had the registration form and check for the 2007 Antarctic Marathon in my pocket.

During the daylong trip (8AM to 5PM), we visited several beautiful waterfalls. I'm happy that I had my binoculars. This included a trip to the Numinbah Valley's "Natural Bridge/Arch Waterfall." Fortunately, the area had an unseasonably high rainfall. The flooding resulted in some beautiful waterfalls.

Running Shoes Are Cheaper Than Insulin

We had lunch at a restaurant in the forest. The tour group was able to feed Rainbow Lorikeet birds. The tour guide spread jelly on pie pans for the birds to lick off. The birds were so used to people that they actually landed on the pans while people were holding them. Some people had three or four birds on their pans, a bird on each shoulder, and one on their head. It was amazing.

On our return trip, we passed through a town called Murwillumbah. This town is known for sugar cane. The heavy downpours actually caused the cane fields to be flat. We also stopped at the Tropical Fruit World for about an hour. They grow thousands of fruit and try to adapt them for the Australian climate.

Last night, I had dinner at a Thai restaurant near the hotel. Unfortunately, I couldn't eat all of the food. The prawn was good, but they didn't have tartar sauce or shrimp sauce. I guess I should have asked for ketchup.

This morning, I went for a 30-minute run along the shoreline trail. Afterwards, I actually put my bare feet in the South Pacific Ocean. I spent most of the day exploring the malls and shopping centers that are south of the hotel. I also got my finisher's medal engraved to commemorate my 50th birthday's accomplishment.

This evening, I'll be having dinner at the Food Fantasy Restaurant and attend the "Midnight Magic Show" at the Conrad Jupiter Casino.

Written 12:15 PM, July 6 on the return flight home

Last night, I attended the magic show at the casino. It was a good and relaxing way to end the trip. Upon my return, I continued packing for the return trip. I decided to stay up late and watch the Tour de France.

I really lucked out on the plane ride. I got a row to myself!!! Another passenger asked me for the window seat and I agreed. This is such a relief!!!

Sahara, *Fever Pitch*, and *Million Dollar Baby* were the movies watched during the flight. I also watched *A Boy Among Polar Bears* and *The Challenge: North Pole*.

Post-Trip Events

I returned to Dallas and was undecided about whether or not to remain married. I entered the house and no one was home. They knew when I would be arriving. I went through the mail. Since I didn't see a birthday card from my wife, I decided to leave.

As I was packing, I realized that I had accumulated t-shirts from over 75 races, some of which had barely been worn. I decided to get 24 of them made into a quilt and donate the rest to the homeless shelter.

A year later, the divorce was finalized. I found myself referring back to the quote from A Gathering of Old Men. It read, "Sometimes you got to hurt something to help something. Sometimes you have to plow under one thing in order for something else to grow."

Lessons Learned

- Don't be afraid to ask other people to take my photo.
- Offer to trade a window seat for an aisle seat on the airplane.
- Take a small DVD player with extra battery packs. (While a laptop may have a larger screen, you may not

be able to open it fully when the seat in the front is reclined.)
- Loosen my seat belt on flights to prevent feeling "strapped in."
- Take walks during long flights and stretch every hour.
- Buy luggage with wheels.
- Read the travel guide BEFORE I get on the plane to minimize any last minute shocks.
- Carry a saltshaker.

ASIA (CHINA) - GREAT WALL MARATHON

Date: May 20, 2006
Marathon Number: 77
International Marathon Number: 4
Inspirational Song: "Once In A Life Time" performed by The Talking Heads

Running Shoes Are Cheaper Than Insulin

Race Selection Process

I applied for the 2007 Antarctica Marathon in July of 2005. This was around my 50th birthday in Australia. Marathon Tours and Travel out of Boston was the exclusive agency for the Antarctica race. I was immediately placed on the wait list. I noticed that the agency also booked other marathon tours. I reasoned that if I signed up for another marathon through them, then I may be moved up on the wait list.

Since I had managed to survive the long plane flights to and from Australia, I decided to sign up for the Great Wall of China Marathon (GWCM). About a month after they received my GWCM deposit, I was taken off of the Antarctica Marathon wait list and was reserved a spot for 2007.

Initially, I signed up for the one-week tour. However, I realized that this might be the only opportunity to visit this country. Therefore, I decided to take the extended two-week tour and cruise. Subsequently, it was the absolute best travel decision that I had ever made.

The GWCM was the first time that I travelled as part of a tour group as an adult. The only other time was in April of 1968. My mother was the principal's secretary at the predominately Black, Soldan High School in St. Louis. She was a chaperon for the high school's senior trip. My brother and I accompanied her on the trip. We were in the ninth and eighth grades, respectively. The first scheduled stop of the East Coast tour was Washington, DC.

Unfortunately, Dr. Martin Luther King, Jr. was assassinated a couple of days before we departed. We arrived in Washington only to see it being patrolled by the National Guard. Some of our scheduled tours were cancelled because we were Black. We also had to adhere to a curfew. The last time that Washington was patrolled by the Guard was during the Civil War. So, this was a historic event to experience and witness.

The events leading up the 2006 GWCM tour were just as turbulent as it was before the 1968 senior trip. Only it was much more personal. My simple divorce had turned very nasty. Although there weren't any children involved (they were adults) and there weren't a lot of assets (only a house and retirement accounts), my wife insisted on trying to make my life miserable.

The divorce hearing was set for a couple of weeks after I returned. I had real concerns about whether or not I would even be able to go on the trip. However, thanks to help and encouragement from some friends, I boarded the flight for China. I had resolved not to let anyone control my happiness.

Prior to the trip, I had purchased another digital camera. This replaced the one that broke during the 2005 Australian trip. I had also purchased a water bottle belt and a used laptop computer. The belt was later referred to as my "Batman Utility Belt." It carried two full-size water bottles and had two pockets. The camera was small enough to fit in one of the pockets. I carried food, money, passport, medical info, and toilet paper in the other pocket.

Since I wanted to keep my friends and relatives up to date on my adventures, I decided to build a website with my daily activities and related photos. My laptop allowed me to download photos from my camera, make a backup copy using flash drives, and build a MS Front Page website nightly.

Running Shoes Are Cheaper Than Insulin

This process allowed me to organize my photos before I returned to the US. I envisioned myself trying to find the time to sort through and organize over a thousand photo images a week after returning. I also envisioned myself losing or damaging the camera and related images. The travel logs eliminated my problems.

When the first web pages were created, there were about 20 people reading them daily. By the end of the trip, there were several hundred readers. As word about the website spread throughout the tour group, they sent the links to their relatives and friends. I found myself corresponding with their relatives and other readers. It was great. Here are edited versions of our daily adventures.

Travel Log

Tuesday, May 16 - DFW/Chicago/Beijing Arrival

Monday, May 15 10:34 PM Dallas/Tuesday, May 16 11:34 AM China

We departed Dallas on time to reach our connecting flight in Chicago. Naturally, I watched the George Clinton/Parliament DVD. Much to my surprise, there were four other Dallasites on the plane who were going to the races.

I really lucked out on the Chicago to Beijing flight. I was stuck with a window seat and was unable to switch seats. The plane was completely full. However, I was able to switch seats with a young couple and secured an aisle seat. Yes!!!! I've learned my lessons from the Australian trip. I walk around after every movie or 45 minutes to stretch my legs. I'm also staying well hydrated. We watched "The Interpreter" and "The Transporter II."

I set my watch to China time prior to departure. I didn't realize that although China is a large country, they use only one time zone. I've spent the last hour updating the CPA website with the photos from the George Clinton concert and my birthday party. When I arrive at the hotel, I'll attempt to update the website and send email messages. My objective is to spend a little bit of time each evening uploading photos and updating this log.

Monday, May 15 4:30 AM Dallas / Tuesday, May 16 5:30 PM China

I just checked into the hotel room. Much to my surprise, they have the same power switch in the room as the hotel in Denmark. As soon as you enter the hotel room, there's a slot by the door. When you insert the room key (plastic card), it turns on the power to the room. This helps to lower their energy bill because people can't walk out and leave the TV running. However, you can't let your laptop, DVD, and other equipment charge up while you're away during the day. You have to charge it at night.

All of us are worn out. However, we have an 8:15 meeting and dinner.

Monday, May 15 7:30 AM Dallas/Tuesday, May 16 8:30 PM China

Our meeting was very interesting. We depart to inspect the race course on Thursday at 5AM!!! We depart for the actual race at 3AM on Saturday!!! Folks, this isn't a vacation...It's a job. I thought that I'd get to "sleep in" at least one morning. I guess I'll take a vacation when I return to work. :-)

We had a good dinner. The group from D/FW was joined by a British coupleat dinner. The British gent took up running marathons when he retired a few years ago. As it turns out, we'll both be running the Antarctic Marathon together.

Tomorrow, we visit Tian An Men Square, the Forbidden City's Imperial Palace, and the Temple of Heaven. I found a McDonald's within walking distance of the hotel. Naturally, as a one-share shareholder in McDonald's, I'll have to experience a Chinese Big Mac. This has become one of my Seven Continent minor goals...to taste a Mickey D's on each continent.
TTFN...Tony

Wednesday, May 17 - Beijing

Wednesday, May 17 8:45 AM Dallas/Wednesday, May 17 9:45 PM China

Here are some photos from Tian An Men Square, the Forbidden City, the Temple of Heaven, and dinner. Our day started at 7AM for breakfast and ended at 9:30 PM. Needless to say we did a lot of walking. However, it was well worth it. During our dinner/banquet, I found myself actually eating Peking duck for the first (and last) time.

On Thursday, we must awake at 4AM to catch our 5AM bus to the Great Wall. It's a two-hour drive. Hopefully I'll be able to sleep on the bus.

Our tour guide said that we should not be surprised if people wanted to take our photos. This was especially true if you're a tall, blond-haired, blue-eyed, Caucasian female. Some of the Chinese tourists live in the mountains and countryside and have never seen or touched a Caucasian. Much to my surprise, I was yanked into a group photo. Evidently, a Black man was an even rarer sight.

Running Shoes Are Cheaper Than Insulin

If you look closely, all of the women have gold-plated teeth. Some rappers would have felt at home!!!

Tian An Men Square Photos

China National Museum - This outdoor clock shows the countdown to the 2008 Olympics.

Great Hall of the People - My blue water bottle is actually a water purification system. It cleans the tap water so it becomes drinkable.

Monument to the People's Heroes

Forbidden City Photos (from the front to the back)

Running Shoes Are Cheaper Than Insulin

Forbidden City Entrance and Mao (View from Tian'an Men Square)

Gate of Supreme Harmony (Outside)

Hall of Supreme Harmony (Inside)

Marble Carriageway

Hall of Preserving Harmony

Running Shoes Are Cheaper Than Insulin

Gate of Heavenly Purity

Pavilion of a Thousand Autumns

The Temple of Heaven (better known as Tian Tan)

The emperor would come to the Temple of Heaven to make sacrifices and pray.

Inside Courtyard

This is the actual spot atop the Round Altar where the Emperors stood and prayed for good harvests.

Running Shoes Are Cheaper Than Insulin

Qinian Dian - The Emperor prayed here for a good harvest.

Dinner

Thursday, May 18 - Beijing, Great Wall Tour, and McDonald's

Thursday, May 18 5:45AM Dallas/Thursday, May 18 6:45PM Beijing

We arose at 4AM to catch buses for the three-hour drive to Huangyaguan. This is the town for the start/finish line of the Great Wall (GW) Marathon. Bag breakfasts were provided for us. There was a collective "wow" as we saw the GW for the first time. It was awe-inspiring, breathtaking, and oh so cool. We made our way to the Yin Yang Square. This is a small arena.

We listened to the race director provide information about the race. He said that, in total, there were about 1200 people for the full and half marathons: 10K, and 5K. There were about 450 marathoners and 360 half marathoners. They've arrived here from all over the world. I counted no more than seven.

Our objective for the day was to walk on the GW for approximately 3.5 kilometers (2.1 miles). This is the same route that we'll be running on Saturday. Half marathoners will run this route once. The marathoners must run it twice.

This was very, very emotional. You start by experiencing pure excitement. You're taken in by the natural beauty around you and gain a great amount of respect for the wall builders. I tried to take photos that show the beauty of the countryside and the condition of the trail.

The more you walk, the more you begin to question the sanity of the people who laid out the course and your personal sanity for actually wanting to run the marathon on it. You accept the fact that either you're totally crazy or very adventuresome. I've accepted the fact that I'm a little of both.

At times, the wall is crumbing and very, very steep and narrow. Unfortunately, there were 100 feet drop offs without a rail to hold on to. The steps are uneven. We were told that the marathoners would run up and down over 3,000 (yes, THREE THOUSAND) steps!!!

You really have to focus or you'll fall. They recommended that you not pass anyone while on the stairs and you leave about 3 feet of space between you and the next person. Naturally, there were some idiots who insisted on passing people on the stairs and by the drop offs anyway.

We're hoping that it doesn't rain. It will make the GW one huge, slippery mess. We also recognized that it will be impossible to run on the wall. My co-runners and I decided to walk on it. In order to maintain our focus, we'll have to be well hydrated before we get to the wall and only drive fluids in the guard towers. Dehydration could lead to dizziness and a very long and hard fall. Navigating the GW will be very serious business.

It took about 1.5 hours to walk the GW and take photos. It was a very humbling experience. Immediately afterwards, our legs were literally shaking from the stress. I overheard a race official saying that a lot of people are dropping down to run the shorter races. Even people,who had planned to walk the 5K (3.1 miles) withdrew from their race. They said that once was more than enough. The bus ride back to Beijing was silent. My objective tonight is to get a good night's sleep.

Upon returning, I went to McDonald's. I'm very pleased to announce that a Big Mac, fries, and drink taste exactly like the one's in the US. Tomorrow I'll try Pizza Hut.

First view of the Great Wall of China

Running Shoes Are Cheaper Than Insulin

The Official Entrance of the Great Wall - Notice the NBMA t-shirt.

Long and steep drop offs.

We had to run on this steep, winding trail to get to and from
the Great Wall during the race.

Running Shoes Are Cheaper Than Insulin

McDonald's in Beijing. A Big Mac tastes just like home.

The Beijing New World Shopping Mall near the hotel.

Friday, May 19 - Summer Palace, Pearl Market, Tibetan Lama Monastery, Pre-Race Pasta Dinner

Friday, May 19 4:00 AM Dallas Time/Friday, May 19 5:00 PM Beijing

This has been a busy day. Most of the talk on the bus has been about the marathon course. Our thighs are still hurting from yesterday's walk on the Wall. And to think, tomorrow we have to run over 10 miles and then walk on the Wall.

To make matters worse, the marathoners must repeat this process twice!!! The heat won't make this any easier. However, we agreed that we didn't travel this far to quit before the race even started.

Our day started by visiting the Summer Palace. The interesting part was seeing the "Stone" boat. It's really a wooden boat that's painted to resemble marble or granite.

Afterwards, we went to the Pearl Market to learn about fresh water oysters and pearls. Naturally, we were given

Running Shoes Are Cheaper Than Insulin

an opportunity to shop. We also had a group lunch nearby.
After lunch, we rode to the Tibetan Lama Monastery.
Later this evening, we're having our pasta loading party. I'll
add those photos later. Unfortunately, the party is over
around 8 PM and we get our wakeup call at 2AM for our
3AM departure.

The lack of sleep would not have been a problem 30 years
ago. However, running a marathon on five or six hours
sleep after a two-and-a-half hour bus ride will add to the
challenge. Hopefully, I'll be able to sleep on the bus ride to
the marathon.

Summer Palace Photos

It's believed that writing the symbols on the ground leads
to a long life.

Notice that each window has a different shape.

A courtyard entrance.

Running Shoes Are Cheaper Than Insulin

The 17-Arch Bridge. The emperors were very number oriented. The number nine was a royal number. In the palaces, it wasn't unusual to see doors with nine rows of nine "bumps." This bridge has 17 arches because the middle arch represents the ninth arch as you count the arches from either the left or right.

A pavilion in the Summer Palace.

Pearl Market

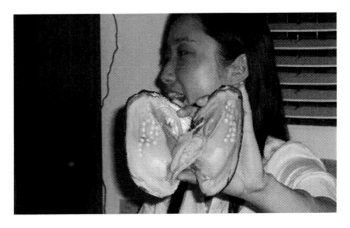

Fresh water oysters have about 20 pearls. I did not buy any pearls!!! However, I obtained an interesting gift. It's based on the James Bond movie with Halle Berry. Ironically, the salesperson's ID number was "007."

The Tibetan Lama Monastery

We passed the construction of the 2008 Olympic Stadium on our way to the monastery.

Running Shoes Are Cheaper Than Insulin

This is the front gate. The plaque spells "peace" in Manchu, Tibetan, Mandarin, and Mongolian.

The "Smiling Buddha" Temple. Believers will burn incense and pray at each temple.

This statute represents where you'll be in death. The higher your coin lands, the closer to heaven you'll be in death. I didn't toss a coin.

A lion and lioness always guard the entrance to royal locations. The lioness is always on the left. A lion cub is always under her left paw. This represents her reproductive capabilities. The male lion always has a ball under his right paw. This represents the world.

I have to lay out my clothes, pin on my race numbers, and prep for tomorrow's race. I'll be too tired after this evening's dinner to focus properly. I'll be carrying my camera with me throughout the race. Those photos will be posted tomorrow evening, along with this evening's pre-race pasta party photos. Wish me luck.

Running Shoes Are Cheaper Than Insulin

Saturday, May 20 - The Great Wall of China Marathon

Saturday, May 20 5:00 PM Dallas/Sunday, May 21 6:00 AM Beijing

It's 6AM the day after the marathon. I've been up since 5:30 revamping the China trip web pages while listening to and watching 2004 George Clinton's concert. For those who don't know me, this is an indication that I'm in a very, very good mood. I changed the website to allow even faster loading of the photos.

These photos are in sequential order from the start of the day until the end. I tried to take photos that show the changes in the running trail and different views from the trail. I'd like to thank the runners and race helpers who took my photo during the race.

A Special Message to the Non-Runners

This was the absolute toughest marathon I've ever run. This was my 77th marathon or ultra-marathon. A number of other veteran runners concurred. To help put this in perspective, my worst marathon (26.2-miles) finishing time was 5 hours, 45 minutes. This occurred in a marathon where the temperatures exceeded 100 degrees. I've also run a 50K (31.1-mile) ultra-marathon in 7 hours. It took me 7.5 hours to finish The Great Wall Marathon (GWM)!!!

The race started "flat" and proceeded up a long, steep hill on asphalt. Next, we entered the Great Wall area. Here, we encountered over 3,500 steps. These were of various heights. At times, we were walking along ledges. Again, most of these areas were too steep to run either up or down. However, the scenery was beautiful.

After departing the main section of the wall, we proceeded down a steep dirt trail. It was actually too steep for most of us to run down. Again, to help put this in perspective, it took me two hours to run the first six miles. This compares to one hour under normal circumstances.

Over 100 photos were taken during the race. This was the first time I've taken photos during a race. This gave me an excuse to stop and take a much-needed rest. (Years later, this will be my excuse for not running the race any faster.)

Throughout the marathon, there were a number of cynical and sarcastic signs along the road. They were usually strategically placed. I couldn't help but take these pictures. (I didn't have to ask the signs to stand still!!!)

On the bus at 3 AM

Running Shoes Are Cheaper Than Insulin

The runners were met by a band (in the flatbed truck) and dancers.

In the arena at the start of the marathon.

The start of the first major hill to get to the Great Wall.

Running Shoes Are Cheaper Than Insulin

The sign says it all.

A major hill & the entrance to the Great Wall

Running Shoes Are Cheaper Than Insulin

Please run slowly,
someone is waiting for you.

Me at the Great Wall and the sign that greeted us.

The start of running on the Great Wall.

A view from The Wall. This gives some perspective about how far we had to go.

Running Shoes Are Cheaper Than Insulin

One of the first ledges. Note the drop off and no railing.
OSHA would have issues with the contractor.

The steep stairs and another ledge. If you think this is difficult in the beginning, the marathoners had to repeat this process AFTER running over 20 miles!!!

Running Shoes Are Cheaper Than Insulin

I'm smiling because my first pass of the wall is over.
However, the steep dirt trail begins.

Some things get lost in translation. We never figured out the meaning of the sign. This kept us from thinking about our pain.

Running Shoes Are Cheaper Than Insulin

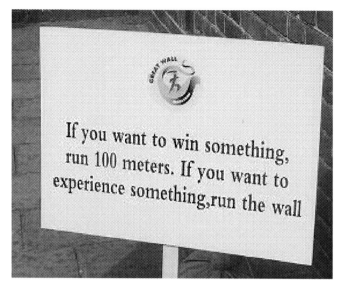

If you want to win something, run 100 meters. If you want to experience something, run the wall

Thank goodness we didn't have to run through the maze.

Beautiful scenery and a rocky farm road.

Running Shoes Are Cheaper Than Insulin

I was as much an "attraction" in the small villages as in Beijing. A non-English speaking runner motioned for me to join the group of children in this photo.

We passed numerous beehives along the way.

We had to run to the white tower in the background.
(Another hill!!!)

We had too much caffeine during the race.

Running Shoes Are Cheaper Than Insulin

After running on asphalt, we switched back to a dirt road.

Scenes of me on the road and at 29K (17.98 miles). I'm smiling because posing gives me a chance (excuse) to rest.

Having successfully made my way back to the arena, I had
to go back up the steep trail to get to the wall again. (By
the way, the word "steep" is not overused in any of the
descriptions!!!)

The bridge-like structure in the middle of this photo is the
arena. You can't have a fear of heights and run this race.

Running Shoes Are Cheaper Than Insulin

From the same spot in the previous photo, this shows how much of the wall I still have to cover. Yes, I have to go to the second guard tower!!!

Excuse the puns from Michael Jackson. I'm "Off the Wall" and I stopped because I got enough.

Back at the arena where I started seven hours, twenty-eight minutes, and forty-five seconds later.

The race ended with a well-deserved shower and massage.

Running Shoes Are Cheaper Than Insulin

Sunday, May 21 - The Drum Tower, Native Lunch, Tea Room, Post-Race Banquet

Sunday, May 21 9:00 PM Dallas/Monday, May 22 10:00 AM China

I'm writing this on our flight to Xian. We awoke around 5:30 and departed the hotel an hour later. Yesterday, we were still recovering from the excitement of finishing the races. The most frequently asked question was, "How do your legs/thighs feel?" We were all in good spirits as we realized that we had just had a once-in-a-lifetime experience.

- Been there.
- Done that.
- Don't want to do it again!!! (At least the running part.)

The day started off with a tour of the Beijing Drum Tower. This is like their version of London's Big Ben. Only this is much, much older. Next, we took a walking tour through an old part of the city. I couldn't help but photograph the bicycle repair shops for the bike riders to view.

We then rode rickshaws through the narrow streets to have a homemade lunch at a local residence. We talked with the husband, wife, and tour guide about their life. This was very, very interesting.

They said that thanks to their Open Door policy, they've learned that there's a difference between the American people and American politicians. The people are friendly, warm, and caring. Enough said.

We rode rickshaws back to the Drum Tower and boarded buses for the teahouse. After sampling the various teas (i.e. onlong, black, jasmine, and white), we returned to the hotel. Several people went to the market for knock-off bargains. While others remained at the hotel or went walking, I updated the website while watching the George Clinton DVD.

The banquet was great. It was held in Beijing's first 5-star hotel. There were over 1,000 runners from 35 countries. I finished 261 out of 272 and 27th in my age group. As best, we can tell everyone from the Marathon Tours completed their event. My final time was 7 hours, 28 minutes, and 45 seconds and 101 stops for photographs!!!

The Drum Tower

Running Shoes Are Cheaper Than Insulin

A view of the Bell Tower from the top of the Drum Tower. The Drum Tower was built during the Kublai Khan era.

Needless to say, it seems that after running up and down 3,500 steps yesterday, the LAST thing we wanted to see were more steep steps.

Street scenes from the Hutong area. This has been a traditional neighborhood for 800 years. Notice the bar's name..."Shut Up, Just Drink."

Running Shoes Are Cheaper Than Insulin

Here are a couple of bike repair shops.

Native Lunch in the Hutong Section

We ate lunch in the traditional Hutong living quarters. We returned to our bus in the rickshaws.

Post-Race Banquet

Running Shoes Are Cheaper Than Insulin

Monday, May 22 - Beijing to Xian flight, Tang Luncheon, Wild Goose Pagoda (12th Century), City Protective Wall and Gates.

Monday, May 22, 4:15 AM Dallas Time/Monday, May 22, 5:15 PM Xian

Flight from Beijing to Xian

Lunch at the Tang Dynasty.

The Wild Goose Pagoda.

Running Shoes Are Cheaper Than Insulin

As usual, in order for us to get to the top, we had to climb steep stairs, again.

Ringing this bell is supposed to bring good luck.

The Xian City Wall

This was originally built to protect the city from its enemies. In the 1960s and 1970s, the citizens removed the bricks and used them for their homes. Parts of the wall were later restored using these same bricks.

Running Shoes Are Cheaper Than Insulin

Tuesday, May 23 - The Terra-Cotta Warriors, Provincial
Historical Museum, and the Tang Dynasty Theatre

***Wednesday, May 24 10:30 AM China/Tuesday, May 23
9:30 PM Dallas***

Yesterday, May 23, started with a trip to see the Terra-
Cotta, human-sized clay warriors. These were discovered
by a farmer who was digging a well in 1974. We were able
to purchase a booked, which was autographed by the
farmer.

We also purchased certified replicas of the warriors made
using the same clay. There are currently three pits, which
contain over 7,000 soldiers, archers, and horses. The clay
warriors are life-sized and made over 2,200 years ago. We
were awe-struck.

Running Shoes Are Cheaper Than Insulin

Next, we went to Xian's Provincial Historical Museum. We were able to see other relics from over 2,000 years ago. I must be considered an (old) relic. I was stopped twice by strangers to take photos with the Chinese. I may start charging people to have my photo taken!!!

We toured a jade factory and (of course) shopped.

Running Shoes Are Cheaper Than Insulin

We finished the day with dinner and a show at the Tang Dynasty Theatre. The meals were fantastic. Unfortunately, I packed the menu away so I can't list the courses. The entertainers played ancient instruments and performed various dances.

This morning, we must have our luggage (to be checked) outside our doors at 9:30. Our bus departs for the airport around noon. We're heading to Chongqing, China's old capital city during World War II.

After dinner, we'll board the Victoria Queen for a three-night cruise up the Yangtze River to see the Three Gorges. We'll stop in Shibaozhai, Gengdu, or Wanzhoe. I'm not sure whether I'll have Internet access. So, this may be my last transmission until our arrival in Shanghai on Sunday.

Running Shoes Are Cheaper Than Insulin

Wednesday, May 24 thru Saturday, May 26 - Yangtze River Cruise, Three Gorges, and Related Stops

Thursday, May 25 10:30 AM China/Wednesday, May 24 9:30 PM Dallas

It rained for the first time since our trip. However, it couldn't have picked a better day. Our morning was free time so we could sleep late or be adventuresome and walk around Xian. We had lunch at a local restaurant and departed for the airport. We couldn't help but notice that all our restaurants have gift shops at the entrance or exit.

We had a good flight from Xian to Chongqing. It lasted about an hour. We boarded buses and headed to the Chongqing Marriott Hotel for dinner. Our tour guide pointed out that Chongqing is a located in the mountains. Thus, unlike Beijing and Xian, we won't see many bicyclists.

They use cars and public transportation systems to move about.

The restaurant served a "Western" buffet. So, we were able to eat pizza and pasta, along with Chinese food. The Marriott was in the process of building an even taller hotel next to the existing facility. After dinner, we left for the Victoria Queen Cruise Ship. It was about a ten-minute drive from the hotel.

As we approached the ship, a band started playing. The rooms were nice, if you we're shorter than six feet. Unfortunately, the fog/haze from the much-needed rain left very few good photo opportunities.

This morning, we have a couple of optional events to attend: a lecture about the Yangtze River and Chinese medical practices. We've been discussing whether or not the US medical professionals will be able to make the trip a tax deductible event and get training credits by attending the one-hour seminar.

The Yangtze River is the world's third largest river behind the Nile and Amazon. The dam is being built for flood control and to generate power.

Running Shoes Are Cheaper Than Insulin

Nighttime views of Chongqing from the ship.

Running Shoes Are Cheaper Than Insulin

Thursday, May 25 5:30 PM/Thursday, May 25, 4:30 AM

The weather is very humid and warm. Unfortunately, I'm unable to take good scenery photos due to the fog.

The ship docked at a small city named Feng Du on the Yangtze. The city was actually moved and rebuilt across the river. This city is known as Ghost City. In the Eastern Han Dynasty, a couple of officials, Wang Pang Ping and Ying Chang Sheng, decided to leave the city life for the countryside. Subsequently, they settled on Mt. Minshan.

It's believed that when Ping and Sheng died, they became immortal. Since their surnames, Ying and Wang, sound like "King of Hell" in Chinese, people began calling Feng Du the Ghost City. Thus, the temples on My. Minshan depict images of life in hell.

Feng Du - The Ghost City

We had the option of riding up the mountain in a cable car or walking up the 700 steps. Since many of us had not run since the Great Wall Marathon, we opted for the steps!!!

There were three different temples. If you successfully passed the three ritualistic tests, you may select either to live a long life or become wealthy. This bottom photo shows a structure with three bridges. You cross over the middle bridge to get to the first temple. On your return trip, after going through the three temples, you walk across the left bridge for longevity or the right bridge for wealth.

Running Shoes Are Cheaper Than Insulin

Our boat docked in front of the local racetrack.

Friday, May 26 5:30 PM China/Friday, May 26 4:30 AM Dallas

Today started earlier than usual. The Victoria Queen entered the first of the Three Gorges, the Qutang Gorge, around 6:45AM on the Yangtze River. The visibility was hazy and misty. Around 8:30, we docked at Wushan and took a ferryboat up/down the Daning River to the Mini Three Gorges. We were able to spot wild moneys, a hidden casket, and various rock formations.

At one time, this river was so small and shallow that a boat couldn't float down it. There's a photo in a book that shows the original city of Wushan. It's now completely under about 50 meters of water. It was moved across the river to higher ground to New Wushan.

The city of Wushan (above photo) was moved across the river before it was flooded.

The ferryboat docked and we switched to smaller sampans. We then went through smaller gorges along the Madu River, a tributary of the Daning. The sampans and the other entertainers were farmers who lost land as a result of the river flooding their farmland. We made our way back to the Victoria Queen and proceeded to the Wu Gorge, the second gorge, and the Xiling Gorge, the third and last gorge.

Scenes from the Qutang Gorge, The First Gorge.

Running Shoes Are Cheaper Than Insulin

Madu River Scenes (Mini Three Gorges) from the Sampan

Running Shoes Are Cheaper Than Insulin

Entrance to the Wu Gorge, The Second Gorge.

A presentation by David, the snuff bottle painter. I purchased a couple of his vases.

Entrance to the Xiling Gorge, The Third and Final Gorge.

Saturday, May 27 11:00 AM China/Friday, May 26 10:00 PM

Last night, we docked at the Yichang District port. This city is the location of the older Gezhou Dam and the newer, still under construction, Three Gorges Dam at Sandouping. Sandouping is about 24 miles from Yichang. Once at the dam site, we saw the power station, which is partly under construction.

We were told that its construction uses a significant amount of the world's concert. We concluded our trip by visiting the Jar Hill Observation Platform and the dam museum.

Our next stop on the cruise ship takes us to the airport for our flight to Shanghai.

Port Entrance

Power Generators

Scenes from The Jar Hill Observation Platform

Running Shoes Are Cheaper Than Insulin

Here are some daytime photos of the dam locks. These better illustrate the water level changes in the dam locks.

We were somewhat excited watching this process. After reading about the Panama Canal Locks in school, it's interesting to actually be in a lock and experience the process first hand.

Our scheduled flight to Shanghai was about three hours late. To help pass the time at the noisy airport, a couple of us watched the DVD Saint Ralph. Since we couldn't hear the movie, we switched to the English subtitles. Thank goodness for technology!!!

Sunday, May 28 - City Tour, Old Shanghai, Yu Yuan Gardens & Shopping Bazaar, Silk Carpet Making Factory, Shanghai Museum area, dinner, and the Huangpu River Cruise.

Sunday, May 28 11:00 PM China/Sunday, May 28 10:00 PM Dallas

This has been a long day. We spent our morning going to the Old Town of Shanghai, the Yu Yuan Gardens, and the related Bazaar. We ate lunch at a Mongolian Restaurant. Next, we went to the Shanghai Museum where several interesting building designs were also within view. I ate dinner with the British couple at a restaurant that overlooked the city at nightfall. The skyline views were beautiful. The entire group ended the evening on a Huangpu River Cruise.

Tomorrow is our last day of touring. I think that we've bonded together as a tour group. However, we're looking forward to going home. This has been a great experience and we're looking forward to meeting in other parts of the world.

Running Shoes Are Cheaper Than Insulin

Hotel Room View

Yu Yuan Gardens and Street Bazaar

The Huxingting Teahouse is located in the middle of the old city.

Running Shoes Are Cheaper Than Insulin

This wall is named the Dragon Wall. There are nine humps in the dragon. Nine is the good luck number for the emperor.

Silk Carpet-making Factory

The top photo shows the worker tying the dyed, silk knots on the individual strings. The more knots per inch, the higher the quality and more expensive the product. The

Running Shoes Are Cheaper Than Insulin

worker at the bottom is shaving the carpet to give the appearance of a raised design.

Shanghai Museum Area

It's shaped like a Shang-dynasty bronze ding pot.

Huangpu River Cruise Scenes

These are photos of The Bund in Pudong.

Running Shoes Are Cheaper Than Insulin

The tower is the Oriental Pearl TV Tower in Pudong.

Monday, May 29 - Last Day & Final Dinner

Monday, May 29 11:00 PM China/Monday, May 29 10:00 AM Dallas

Monday started with a 1.5-hour bus ride to the canal city of Suzhou. We toured the Master of Nets Garden. This was followed by a tour of the Suzhou Silk Embroidery Research Institute.

The Silk Embroidery Research Institute

Silk worms at mealtime.

Running Shoes Are Cheaper Than Insulin

This was different from the previous silk tour. We saw the silk weavers using threads that were as thin as a strain of hair. The pictures/patterns that they wove were visible on both sides of the cloth. This was very impressive (and expensive). We concluded the trip with a 45-minute boat ride on the canals.

Running Shoes Are Cheaper Than Insulin

We had our second farewell dinner later that evening at the Shanghai Uncle Restaurant. While the food was good, much of the talk centered on our next international marathons and how we would stay in contact via the Internet. For the record, over 700 photos were taken during this trip. Needless to say, it was impossible to display all them.

It's been fun.

Take care,
Tony

Post Tour Comments

The tour group was very great. One of our tour guides said it best. Since our group was very physically fit, she didn't have to worry about stragglers. We were "game" for just about anything. And we complained very little. Since many of the ancient Chinese structures were built prior to elevators, we spent a lot of time climbing stairs.

I really enjoyed bargaining for souvenirs. I think that I got pretty good at it. I discovered that it was like negotiating for software and hardware.

Four of my Texas "tour mates," a couple from England, and I have since met in other marathons around the world. They were also on the 2007 Antarctica and Argentina tour with Marathon Tours & Travel.

Afterwards, a couple of the runners convinced me to join them on an African tour with Marathon Tours and Travel. We went on to run Kenya's Safaricom Lewa Marathon. It was the final marathon for us in our quest to complete the Seven Continents Goal.

In all, we completed four of our international marathons together. Subsequently, we discovered that a couple of us had unknowingly run the Gold Coast Marathon on July 3, 2005!!! It's a small world.

I had a fantastic time with the tour group and made some life-long friends. I believe that the Internet and email made it possible for us to stay in touch.

This was my first international marathon since my separation. The divorce hearing was scheduled a few weeks after my return. This trip gave me the opportunity to free my mind completely and "de-stress."

Until this trip, my longest vacation was five or six days. I discovered that it took me about four days to forget about my job. Afterwards, I relaxed.

Running Shoes Are Cheaper Than Insulin

Also, after spending so much time focusing on my family's needs, it was strange to think only about myself. I realized that when other people relied on me, I set aside my "gut instinct" and risk taking in favor of logic and caution. I had intentional passed up self-employment business opportunities in favor of working 9 to 5 jobs for other people. If I failed, the entire family suffered. I had to be fiscally conservative.

I recall standing in the silk store holding a beautiful, black and gold, 100 percent pure silk comforter and pillow covers. I was debating whether or not to buy it. I could definitely afford it.

I was so accustomed to discussing purchases with my wife, relying on her interior-design qualities, or taking into consideration our children's activities that I struggled with trusting myself to make the right choice.

Finally, I realized that this may be my ONLY time in China. I never wanted to regret not taking an action when I had the once-in-a-lifetime opportunity. I bought the items. It was the best decision I had made.

From that moment on, my life changed for the better. However, I will admit, this trip would have been more fun with "a significant other."

Lessons Learned
- Tackle every major obstacle one step at a time.
- Get your passport, visas, and shots early.
- Make/scan copies of your travel documents in PDF and html formats. Carry these with you on a flash/jump drive and email them to yourself. Thus, if you lose the documents and jump drives, you may obtain copies from your email account.

- Take two-week vacations.
- Trust my gut instinct.
- Travel with a physically fit tour group.
- Take $100 per person in one-dollar bills for every week of vacation. This is for tips and small purchases.
- Carry a water purification filter system bottle. It's cheaper than purchasing bottled water.
- Buy a really good and new travel guide. Don't buy a used guide because things change quickly between printings. It doesn't make sense to spend $10 on a guide for a $5,000 tour. I used my guide every day.
- Carry a camera during the marathon.

ANTARCTICA MARATHON

Date: February 26, 2007
Marathon Number: 82
International Marathon Number: 5
Inspirational Song:
" A Psychoalphadiscobetabioaquadoloop" performed by Parliament

Race Selection Process

Ever since I read about the Antarctica Marathon and the Seven Continents Club, I wanted to run it. However, I wasn't sure whether or not I could afford the trip. Due to the popularity of the event, it filled up quickly. The 2007 marathon applications became available in the late Spring of 2005.

Marathon Tours & Travel, the sole travel agency for the race, sent me an application. I carried it with me during my Australian, 50th birthday adventure. I read it numerous times on the trip and kept debating whether or not I should send in the deposit.

The day after running Australia's Gold Coast Marathon, I went on the tour of the Hinterlands, a rain forest. It's also known as Lamington National Park.

We visited the "Best of All Lookout." This was located on the lip of the crater rim. The crater is about 80K or 50 miles across. On our way to the lookout point, we saw "Antarctica trees." These are the trees that remained after Australia broke off from Antarctica.

This was déjà vu. During the Birmingham Mercedes Marathon, I was trying to decide whether or not to run Cincinnati's Flying Pig Marathon. A few minutes later, I was running through the "pink pig" decorated neighbor. I went on to run the Flying Pig Marathon a couple of months later. I had a great time.

While looking at the Antarctica tree in Australia, I had the registration form and check for the 2007 Antarctic Marathon in my pocket. I mailed them when I returned to the hotel.

Running Shoes Are Cheaper Than Insulin

The limited number of spots for the trip filled up quickly. I was put on the wait list. However, my application was accepted several months later.

The tour director convinced the Fin Del Mundo race director to change the date of his event to coincide with our arrival from Antarctica. The race is held in Ushuaia, Argentina. Thus, for the cost of an extra couple of nights in a hotel and an entry fee, we could run a South American marathon; A two [continents] for one [plane ticket] treat. Needless to say, I jumped at the chance.

Training Problems

Since Dallas isn't known for its cold temperatures and steep hills, training for the Antarctica weather conditions wasn't easy. I purchased cold weather running clothes. However, it only got cold enough for me to wear everything only one day during the winter.

During the other days, I'd wear one layer at a time. And even one layer of clothing was too warm for Dallas temperatures. I did learn that I had problems keeping my fingers warm. I kept visualizing losing my fingers to frost bite. I love all of my fingers and didn't plan to part with any of them.

Leading up to Christmas, I was monitoring the weather in St. Louis, my hometown. As soon as I saw that they would have several days of sub-freezing temperatures, I decided to spend Christmas there. During my visit, I had an opportunity to go on several training runs and wear all of my layers of clothing.

However, I still had problems with my fingers. Between December and February, I tested various types of mittens, gloves, and mitten/glove combinations, including battery-powered, chemically-warmed, and breath-warmed gloves,

They worked for a short time. Unfortunately, I may be running for up to seven hours. And it may be too cold or difficult to change the batteries or chemical packs or unscrew the air compartment.

I finally solved the problem by wearing layers. I wore a thin glove close to my hand. Next, I wore a glove/mitten that I purchased in Amsterdam. The third layer was a windbreaker mitten cover. It worked out just fine.

Travel Log

This adventure begins with our departure on Feb. 19 and concludes with our arrival on March 9. Unlike the China tour, I may only have Internet access while on land. Thus, between Feb. 23 and March 5, the website may not be updated. However, I'll update the website pages daily. As soon as we dock, I'll upload the photos.

Also, Buenos Aires is three hours ahead of Dallas time. This has been a technological challenge between filling up the memory cards for the camera and running out of space on my laptop. Thus, I spend the evenings deleting photos and moving old photos to jump drives. Also, trying to take photos against a white background confuses the camera's light meter. Thus, a number of photos are overexposed and had to be retouched.

Buenos Aires, Argentina - February 19

The fun started at DFW Airport. At the boarding gate, I ran into my Dallas area "tour mates" from the Great Wall of China Marathon. We were going to stay for both

Running Shoes Are Cheaper Than Insulin

marathons. In true "goal-oriented" fashion, we were already talking about an African marathon. It was a smooth 11-hour flight.

After dinner and a DVD ("V for Vendetta"), I went to sleep and awoke in time for breakfast and the 9:15AM landing. We arrived at the Marriot around 10:30AM and agreed to meet at 1PM for lunch. We also decided to join a group for a dinner and tango show.

Compared to our "cool" 40 degree temperatures, it was a hot and humid 81 degrees. We were joined by another Dallas area runner, who was also with us in China, for lunch. We discussed the possible weather conditions for Antarctica, whether or not to camp out overnight in Antarctica, entering in the kayak races, and possibly going on a ferry ride to Colonia del Sacramento, Uruguay.

We stayed at the Buenos Aires Marriot Plaza Hotel. It's across from the park that has the General Jose de San Martin Monument. At the opposite end of the park is the Isias Malvinas-Falkland Islands Memorial and the Torre Monumental (the British Clock Tower). We also found a McDonald's near the hotel. Thus, I can continue my ongoing international, Big Mac taste test.

After lunch, we explored the neighborhood. We found the Galerias Pacifico Mall. I'm beginning to think that the name "Galleria" means "expensive" in every language. Since most of the postcards and paintings include a couple doing the tango, I'm anticipating a fun evening.

The General Jose de San Martin Monument – He's considered the father of their independence.

The Torre Monumental (the British Clock Tower)

Running Shoes Are Cheaper Than Insulin

We went to the Esquina Carlos Gardel for dinner and a tango show. The late Carlos Gardel was a famous singer. His signature song was "Mi Buenos Aires Querido." When it was sung, people in the audience joined in. The show was great. We saw a lot of different tango styles. They performed to a live band.

Goodnight!!!

Buenos Aires, Argentina - February 20

I'm writing this while watching the "The Simpson's" in Spanish....They're dumb in any language. This morning started off with a buffet breakfast in the hotel. Around 9:30, we left for a bus tour of the city. We saw various buildings and monuments and learned a little about Argentina's history.

It has a large European influence from the Spanish and Italians. Our tour guide pointed out that there were very few Blacks in Argentina. Evidently, right before they ended slavery, the owners sold their slaves to Brazil to avoid losing money!!! This also helps to explain Brazil's large Black population.

Running Shoes Are Cheaper Than Insulin

We stopped at the Recoleta Cemetery to visit Evita Peron's burial site. They say that you either love her or hate her. The poor, middle class, and women tend to love her for lifting them up by taking from the rich and giving to the poor. She also worked to give women the right to vote. The elite upper class hated her because they felt that she took their money and used it for herself.

Evita Peron's Family Tomb

They said that the bodies are entombed without any embalming fluids. This causes the body to decay. After about twenty years, family members return to the crypt to remove the bones from the casket. The bones are then placed in a much smaller casket.

The larger one may be reused by another family member. (The family members may pay someone else to remove the bones.) This is an Italian ritual. The cemetery was full of cats. They're fed by the locals. There was a slight odor to the place.

We lost a couple of tourists at the cemetery and continued our trip without them. Next, we headed to a street shopping district to buy souvenirs.

Running Shoes Are Cheaper Than Insulin

Yes, that's me in my multi-pocket, fly fishing vest again. It's like my AmEx card: I don't leave home without it!!!

Running Shoes Are Cheaper Than Insulin

We returned to the hotel around 1:00PM. The rest of the afternoon was our "free time." As we departed for lunch, we ran into the British couple. They were with our group in China last year. They joined us for lunch.

Later that day, I decided to venture out into the shopping district and had a McDonald's Number 1 combo, a Big Mac meal. Based on my taste buds, it was the same as a US Big Mac.

This evening, we had the reception at 6:30. It was followed by a banquet and Q&A session. There's a camera crew from Capella University who will be following the race.

The reception afforded me additional opportunities to talk with runners about their goals, challenges, and their reasons for being in this race. The one comment that was repeated was that people felt good to be surrounded by other achievers. It was like an adrenaline-feeding frenzy.

Our dinner table consisted of my American and British running buddies from The Great Wall of China. We were joined by two interesting women:

- The first woman has run this event three times and completed a marathon on all seven continents.
- The second woman is trying to become the first woman to complete a marathon AND climb the tallest peaks on all seven continents. She's attempted Mt. Everest twice and has scheduled her third trip for later this year.

Needless to say, we had some very interesting discussions during dinner about everything from altitude sickness in distance running and mountain climbing to performing volunteer work in foreign countries.

After the dinner, the discussion about the race and what to expect began. Here are the interesting comments from the meeting.

- A gentleman will attempt to be the first wheelchair athlete to complete the marathon. This is his second attempt. I recall reading that the ankle-deep mud prevented him during his first attempt.
- There's a 75-year woman from Slovakia competing in the half marathon.

Running Shoes Are Cheaper Than Insulin

- There are about 20 people in the half marathon and 170 in the full marathon. (Thus, I'll be able to finish in the top 200!!!)
- We'll be able to get our passports stamped for China, Russia, Chile, and Uruguay during the race since we'll pass through those Antarctica bases.
- The weather will be our guide. The winds can cause the temperature to drop by 20 degrees in a matter of minutes.
- Thom said that describing Antarctica to someone is like trying to describe colors to a blind person. You have to see it to believe it.
- We were also told that more people pass through the gates of Walt Disney in one hour than there are people who have set foot in Antarctica. We're going to be in an elite group.

Goodnight!!!

Buenos Aires, Argentina - February 21

Today was a "free" day in our tour schedule. Three of us went for a three-mile run this morning. We returned in time for the buffet breakfast. We were joined at our table by a Canadian reporter from the Yukon. He's writing a story for *Men's Journal* about running his first marathon. He picked one interesting race for his first one.

After getting cleaned up, several of us went for a walk in the city. We agreed that since we'd be on a ship for about ten days, we should take advantage of our time on shore. We walked from our hotel to the zoo. This was approximately three miles. Our discussions focused on everything from children to politics and, of course, running.

I took a series of photos at the zoo for Jaden. He's a preschooler. This gave me an opportunity to test out a new camera lens, so bear with me.

After lunch, we walked back to the hotel. Along the way, we passed a number of monuments and the Hard Rock Cafe.

Running Shoes Are Cheaper Than Insulin

The Museo Nacional de Bellas Artes (National Museum of Fine Arts)

The Falkland Islands Memorial

Part of our tour group leaves at 3:30AM (yes, that's AM) to catch flights to Ushuaia. The rest of us leave a day later. So, I'll have a free day tomorrow. Hopefully, I'll go across the river to Colonia, Uruguay. We tried to go yesterday, however, the ferry was full of carnival partygoers.

That's all for today.
Take care and good night.

Buenos Aires, Argentina - February 22

Apparently, the first group made it to Ushuaia this morning. As they say, "No news is good news." I don't believe we'll see them until the marathon on February 26. This is another "free" day for me to explore the area. I decided to get some extra sleep since I've only averaged a few hours a night.

I walked down Florida Street to get to the Obelisco. Florida Street begins at our hotel. It's a pedestrian street with shops lining both sides. It's about 1.5 miles of pure shopping and eating.

Running Shoes Are Cheaper Than Insulin

I turned onto Corrientes Avenue to find the Obelisco. This street is also lined with shops and live performance theaters. The Obelisco is a smaller version of our Washington Monument. I've also seen this structure in Paris.

There really isn't much shopping to do from my perspective. Their major exports are beef and leather, which sounds a lot like Texas. I returned from my walk and gathered my clothes for the laundry. During lunch on our first day, I spotted their business. I figured that it was

Running Shoes Are Cheaper Than Insulin

cheaper for them to "do the dirty work" than for the hotel or the ship. It cost about $2US to wash and iron one load!!!

While the clothes were being washed, I worked out in the hotel's weight room and updated the website. Unless there's Internet access onboard the ship, this will be my last upload until March 6. The ship is called the Akademik Ioffe.

We'll be onboard for ten days. They've told us that we'll have a chance to camp out in tents overnight on Antarctica and do some kayaking after the marathon. Needless to say, I purchased some disposable, waterproof cameras. Unfortunately, I may not be able to get the photos developed and uploaded until my return to the US.

Take care.

Ushuaia, Argentina - February 23

I started the day in Buenos Aires with a 2:00AM wake-up call. We had to be in the lobby by 3:30 to catch our three-hour flight to Ushuaia. We split up into two groups that left at 5:30 and 6:30. We finally cleared customs and made it to Ushuaia around 11:30AM. I spent the early part of this day with the English couple.

We were on our own until 4:00PM. Since we'll be using the Russian base on Antarctica, we were asked to buy some food and alcoholic drinks as gifts.

Ushuaia is the most southern port city. It's small and quaint. They have their souvenir strip and that's where we spent most of our time. We initially got our passports stamped for both Ushuaia and Antarctica. We were trying to find passport stamps with penguins and whales.

"Fin del mundo" means the end of the world or earth.

Running Shoes Are Cheaper Than Insulin

While we were deciding what to do next, I heard my name called. It was a graduate from my high school in St. Louis. She graduated in 1967. She leads Antarctica and Mt. McKinney expeditions. I graduated with her sister-in-law in 1973.

She also introduced me to Dave Hahn. He has climbed Mt. Everest eight times!!! This was so cool. I think that I'd like to visit (not climb) Mt. Everest just to see it for myself. Or possibly visit the first base camp. I hear that it's around 12,000 feet.

Afterwards, I walked around town. It reminded me of a small ski resort with the snowcapped mountains in the back.

I found a combination whistle, compass, thermometer, and magnifying glass. I wanted the whistle to scare away the birds during the marathon. I can use the compass, if I get lost, and the magnifying glass to heat some water for drinking. :-)

There's a glazier that overlooks the city. Unfortunately, due to global warming, it's melting away.

We cleared customs and boarded the ship, the Akademik Ioffe, about 4:30.

Running Shoes Are Cheaper Than Insulin

I'm in cabin 407. My roommate is an attorney from Germany. He's one of the seeded runners. I just hope to be halfway through by the time he's crossing the finish line. At least he'll be out to the shower by the time I finish.

As a rule, there has to be a fire/lifeboat drill within the first 24 hours of launching. We had our drill before dinner. I made a fashion statement with my "special" cap.

After dinner, I put on my motion-sickness patch. We'll be entering the unpredictable Drake Passage tonight. It can either be a calm as a kitty or as bad as a bulldog with 30-foot waves.

It's about 10:30PM and I'm beat.

Good night.

Running Shoes Are Cheaper Than Insulin

Aboard The Akademik Ioffe (Drake Passage Crossing) - February 24

I awoke around 6:30 this morning after sleeping through the night. I slept like a rock. I remember waking up twice to pick up my necklace off the floor. After talking with other passengers, this may have occurred when we entered the Drake Passage.

This passage is supposed to have the world's roughest seas. It is here where the waters from the Atlantic and Pacific meet along with strong winds. This combination of wind and water leads to high waves. I don't know if the small bed felt great or I was just whipped from waking up a 2:00AM to catch the flight.

I took a shower this morning. The seas were so rough that I had to hold onto the rail and wash with one hand. I accidentally washed off my motion-sickness patch and had to use another one. I'll have to wear a shower cap and not wash behind my ears. I also continued writing the book for about an hour.

Everyone looked woozy at breakfast. I couldn't help but notice the motion sickness patches behind people's ears. I ate a bowl of cornflakes. I was advised against eating the fresh pineapple due to the amount of citric acid and the impact it might have on my stomach.

I attended three different lectures today. The first was about the history of Antarctica. We were told that there's more freshwater in this area than anyplace in the world. If it melted, the oceans would rise by about 19 meters.

We also learned about the possible impact of global warming and the increased amounts of CO_2 on the water, current flows, wildlife, and sea levels. This was pretty much in line with Al Gore's movie, "An Inconvenient Truth." I'd highly recommend seeing this movie before going on this trip.

I took a nap until lunch. Napping appears to be a popular pastime around here. Without any land in sight and little activity, people are napping, watching the ocean for animals, or playing cards. This may also be due to the effects of the motion sickness patches. People are also a little nervous about the race. I feel that my body resistance has taken a nosedive. I'm trying to rest as much as possible.

We ate lunch around 1:00 and the gift shop was officially opened. I purchased an Antarctica key chain and a penguin lapel pin for my runner's quilt. Next, I went to a session about kayaking. I decided to not even attempt this activity based on the guides' comments regarding first-timers. It was a little bit too dangerous. However, the next time I venture this way, I plan to be qualified to give it a try.

The next session focused on the history of this marathon and how we should best prepare for race day. We've been warned that there's no guarantee that the marathon will take place. This depends on the weather and the ship's captain.

If it is bad, we may wait in the harbor for one or two days for it to clear up. If the captain doesn't feel the water is safe, we can't leave the ship. We were also told that they will not hold a marathon onboard the ship. Needless to say, we're all hoping for smooth water and good weather. They're mentally preparing us for the worst while hoping for the best.

Since we cannot have more than 100 people assembling in Antarctica at a time, the race will start with two groups.

Running Shoes Are Cheaper Than Insulin

The first group will consist of the half marathoners, women, and men over 60. The next group (the one I'm in) starts three minutes later.

We've been told to stay on the trail. If we see an animal, we're to stay at least 15 feet away. We were also encouraged to bring an extra pair of running shoes and socks. We may be able to change into these at the halfway point in the race. We should expect ice, mud, and plenty of strong winds.

Next, I packed my camera and went to the captain's deck to see how the ship operates. It was interesting to see the signaling flags were still kept. I assume that if the ship ever lost power, they'd use the low-tech flags.

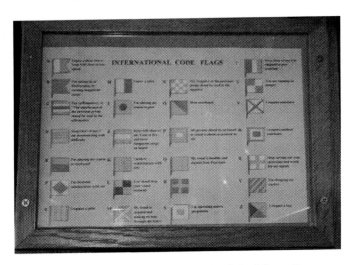

Aboard The Akademik Ioffe (Arrival At King George Island) - February 25

I'm still feeling a little wiped out. I tossed and turned most of the night. So I plan to take it very easy today. We had to attend mandatory sessions about how to get into and out of the zodiacs and race-day preparation. These raft-like boats were designed by Jaques Coustou. He's the guy who did all of the underwater exploration shows when we were kids.

Unlike most marathons, we were advised to take two pairs of running shoes in case we encounter deep mud. We also have to pack post-race clothes to wear back on the zodiac. Furthermore, since we don't know the weather conditions and the weather can change quickly, we need to dress in layers and pack additional warm running clothes.

In a 30-minute period, the winds went from 40 knots to 30 knots. We also have the food and drink gifts for the Russians since they're letting us use their facilities. Many people are concerned about packing.

Running Shoes Are Cheaper Than Insulin

We did learn that there is a very, very small gift shop and a post office at the Chilean Research Facilities. So we have to pack money. Since the Chileans and Argentineans aren't exactly good friends, the Chileans set up a post office to claim their territory. Argentina feels that Antarctica belongs to them; Spain granted them their land and all lands further south.

We also have to wash the soles of our shoes. We're not allowed to bring any dirt from foreign countries. This may contaminate the island. Also, making "yellow snow" is not allowed. They want to keep the environment as pure as possible. We learned that any crimes that we, US citizens, commit in Antarctica may be prosecuted in a US court.

We also received our race numbers after lunch. I'm number 168. My cabin mate, received number 1. This is based on his most recent marathon finishing time. So, he's the top seed in the event. I suspect that while I'm at the halfway point, he'll be finished. On the bright side, we won't have to fight over the shower after the race.

Around 3:00PM, I spotted my first Antarctica animal: a bird. I also saw some penguins swimming in the ocean. Around 4:00PM, we sighted land, Nelson Island!!!

Around 7:00 PM, we found Bellinghausen in Maxwell Bay. This is the sight of the marathon. Also, it's beginning to snow.

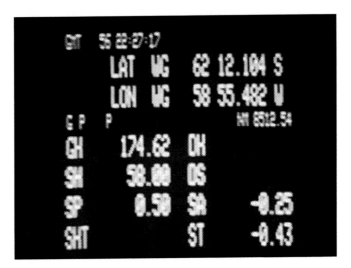

Ship's Map and GPS Location at Bellinghausen

Today, the crew marked the course. We'll have to run through 600 meters of mud four times during the marathon. Since the weather can quickly change, they can't tell us anything about tomorrow's forecast. Thus, we have to pack and dress for the worst possible weather.

Running Shoes Are Cheaper Than Insulin

King George Island, Antarctica, February 26 (Marathon Day)

We were awakened at 6:15 to begin preparation for the marathon. Unlike most marathons, we had to be transported to the starting line by zodiacs. Unlike China's marathon, I was limited in the number of photos that I took. (That translates to a faster marathon finishing time.) With temperatures at or below freezing and 40 mile/hour winds, my fingers froze when I removed my gloves. At one point, I thought that I had frost bite. Another time, I actually dropped the camera in a puddle of water because I couldn't feel it.

The Great Wall of China Marathon is the closet comparison to this marathon. The GWC had man-made obstacles (over 3,400 steps). This one had Mother Nature's obstacles—steep hills and glaciers and weather. The zodiacs had to transport about 200 people from two ships. It took about 15 minutes per trip. We landed at the Russian Research Station called Bellinghausen.

Bellinghausen was an Antarctic explorer. Technically speaking, we were in Russia. Since the course took us through the Uruguay, China, and Chile research stations, we were also in those countries according to the treaties. Antarctica is the only continent without any countries.

You can see from the photos below that we had to bundle up in our waterproof clothes and boots just to be transported to the race site. Also, you'll notice the snowflakes. We had debated about what would be the best conditions; at or below freezing or above freezing.

While we may feel better with the temps above freezing, it would increase the amount of mud we may have to run through. On the other hand, temps below freezing may lead to frost bite.

Running Shoes Are Cheaper Than Insulin

The Russian buildings were situated on stilts. After we landed, we changed into our running gear under the buildings. We left our gear there for the duration of the race. About ten minutes after my zodiac landed, the race started.

The scenery was almost indescribable. It was like looking at a black-and-white photo. With the exception of the runners and man-made objects (i.e. buildings), everything was in shades of gray.

Prior to the trip, I tried running with a face mask. Unfortunately, it was difficult to breathe. So, I grew out my beard. For the first time, the hair on my face was longer than the hair on my head.

My face stayed warm, but my lips lost their feeling. When I drank, I couldn't feel the fluids. I didn't know if it went into my mouth or down my shirt. Also, the anti-fog solution stopped working on my sunglasses and I had to remove

Running Shoes Are Cheaper Than Insulin

them. This created visibility problems since almost everything was white (and getting whiter with the snowfall) and very bright. I had nothing to protect my eyes from the UV rays.

In addition to being cold, Antarctica is very, very dry. After all, it never rains, only snows. Therefore, there's almost no moisture in the air. You have to keep telling yourself that although you're feeling hydrated and not sweating, you must continue to drink fluids.

Did I mention that the "aid stations" are really water bottles tossed in the snow? You find your bottle, take a drink, and put it back in the snow for your return trip. (All of the bottles were retrieved by the support staff after the race.)

The mud fields.

We left the starting line and headed towards the Uruguay Base. Along the way, we ran through ankle deep mud, crossed streams, and climbed many short, steep hills. However, absolutely nothing prepared us for Collins Glacier.

Running Shoes Are Cheaper Than Insulin

It's very difficult to take a photo that shows the challenges of Collins Glacier. The photo below shows the runners on the glacier at a distance.

To help put this in perspective, imagine yourself running on a treadmill at your local gym. After three miles of running, set the angle of the treadmill to 17 percent. (Most treadmills only go to 10 or 12 percent.)

Now, add an icy surface, snow blowing in your face, 40 MPH winds, and no shelter to hide from the wind. Oh, by the way, it's about a 3/4-mile from the glacier's bottom to the turnaround point. Unfortunately, this can't be simulated on a treadmill.

Your calves and thighs ache. Although gravity pulls you downhill, you have to brace for every step so you won't slip and fall. Thus, your thighs are screaming in pain.
Also, if you're running the marathon, you have to do this again around 17 miles!!! Here are a couple of views from the bottom and the turnaround point on the glacier.

Unfortunately, none of these photos really illustrate the difficulty of this part of the course.

View from the bottom of the glacier.

View from the top of the glacier.

Running Shoes Are Cheaper Than Insulin

The glacier was a humbling experience. A number of marathoners decided to quit and just run the half marathon. I actually considered this. However, my thoughts turned to the 3,600 steps that we ran during the Great Wall of China Marathon.

I had to take it one step at a time. Evidently, I would make it to the top. (On my second trip up the glacier, I wore spikes.) I'll never complain about another hill again.

We retraced our steps back to Bellinghausen. The terrain was tough. We ran on lose rock, ice, snow, slush, and mud. Since many of us are also running the Fin Del Mundo Marathon, we were concerned about possible injuries.

We returned to Bellinghausen, ran through the Chilean Base, passed the Russian's Orthodox Church, and headed towards the Chinese "Great Wall" Base. We were told that after the Pope declared that Antarctica was Catholic, the Russians had their church constructed!!! Along the way, we passed "Fur Seal Freeway." As luck would have it, we ran past seals and penguins. I also saw a fellow Texan from the Great Wall of China Marathon. Since we were on different ships, we hadn't seen each other since Argentina.

Running Shoes Are Cheaper Than Insulin

Fur seal on the marathon course.

Russian Orthodox Church.

After we reached the China base, we headed back to Bellinghausen. Half marathoners finished after one loop. However, full marathoners had to go through the loop a second time. This time, there were only a handful of people on the glacier.

So, you really had to concentrate and dig down deep, since there weren't other runners offering encouragement. This actually reminded me of the Great Wall of China Marathon. I had to concentrate on every single step to avoid falling.

This marathon was mentally and physically tough when you combine the weather conditions with the glacier climbs. I finished the marathon within about five minutes of my projected time. Considering the fact that I've been ill the past couple of days, that wasn't bad.

It's 10:30PM and I'm about to pass out. Goodnight.

Running Shoes Are Cheaper Than Insulin

Somewhere Along The West Side Of The Peninsula, Antarctica, February 27

Happy 25th Anniversary!!! My first 26.2-mile marathon was completed on February 27, 1982. I never would have dreamed that I'd be running a marathon in Antarctica. I'm too wiped to do anything but stay in bed. I think that my age has caught up with me. The only time I got out of bed was for bio breaks and food. The other runners went on short excursions in search of whales, seals, and penguins. I was in search of sleep.

This evening's dinner was an outdoor barbeque. Runners from the other ship joined in. The dinner started with the ship's captain performing a wedding ceremony. I grabbed my plate and went back into my warm, comfortable cabin.

They posted the race results. There were 145 marathon finishers and 40 half marathon finishers. A 75-year old lady completed the half marathon. To help put this in perspective, on my February 20 log, we were told that there were about 170 marathoners and 20 half marathoners. The glacier probably caused some of the marathoners to reconsider a second trip. Thus, they switched to the half marathon. We were told that our certificates and medals will be mailed to us upon our return.

I'm wiped out. My thighs and calves are still aching from the race. I'd give anything for a nice massage, hot bath, and a White Castle cheeseburger. I've turned my attention to resting for the Fin del Mundo Marathon. If I complete it, I'll only have to complete an African marathon to join the Seven Continents Club.

Goodnight.

Peterman & Yalour Islands And Lemaire Channel, Antarctica, February 28

I was feeling much better today. Prior to this trip, I "upgraded" my 1975 SLR camera and lenses to a digital SLR model with a couple of zoom lenses. I spent the better part of January getting used to the various features. I had to put all of the skills to use today.

This morning was spent exploring Peterman Island. This island was loaded with Adelie Penguins. This is the molting season. The penguins shed their old feathers as new ones grow in their place. The place has a very bad odor. Imagine thousands of penguins staying in the same place for a few months and their related droppings slowly decaying. Gag!!!

Running Shoes Are Cheaper Than Insulin

This penguin is molting.

We were not allowed to touch any of the animals.
After lunch, we headed to Yalour Island. This island is
inhabited by Gentoo Penguins. Adelie penguins basically
have a black head. Gentoos have more orange on their
beaks and white feathers near their eyes.

Running Shoes Are Cheaper Than Insulin

This is how I felt yesterday!!!

Running Shoes Are Cheaper Than Insulin

While returning from Yalour Island, we decided to scout the area. We thought that this iceberg looked like a whale.

As we approached our ship, we spotted something moving in the water. It wasn't one, but two humpback whales. They were less than 25 yards from us at times.

A whale blowing its spout.

Whenever we returned from the excursions, we had to hose the penguin droppings from our shoes. Many of us are trying to decide whether or not to bring the boots back with us.

After dinner, we turned around and started heading north through the southern end of the Lemaire Channel. It has 3,000-foot peaks.

Running Shoes Are Cheaper Than Insulin

When the packed snow of these peaks break away, they form icebergs. You can see from the photo below that chucks of ice had broken off.

A group of about 60 hardy individuals were to go camping tonight. However, the bad weather forced them to stay onboard the ship.

Goodnight!!!

Neko Harbor, Paradise Bay, And Chilean Air Force Base, Antarctica - March 1

I had a difficult time staying asleep, so I visited the ship's bridge around 5:00AM. The scene was very surreal.

We started the day by cruising in the zodiacs in Neko Harbor. Here's an interesting question, "What happens when a 65-ton, 15-meter long humpback whale meets a small boat full of runners?"

The runners ask the whale to stop and smile for a photo.

This was a very rare opportunity to see two sets of humpbacks in two days. There are only about 3,000 humpback whales left in the world. Needless to say, we spent a lot of time taking photos.

Running Shoes Are Cheaper Than Insulin

Humpback's Face and Hump with Open Month

Two Humpbacks Side-By-Side

After watching and photographing the whales, we turned our attention to the penguins.

After lunch, we went to Paradise Bay. It was loaded with even more penguins. While they look very cute and nice in movies, the odor of their droppings and molting feathers is sickening.

Several people took the opportunity to "swim with the penguins" and joined the Antarctica Swimming Team by getting in the water.

Running Shoes Are Cheaper Than Insulin

Much to our surprise, we were taken to the Chilean Military Station at Waterboat Point.

They had a post office AND a souvenir shop!!! Yes, I could finally purchase some "authentic" Antarctica souvenirs. As luck would have it, they accepted US dollars. I now have an "official" document that shows I was on Antarctica!!!

The Chinese had a similar "directional" sign at their
Antarctic station. There were a couple of men who spent
an entire Antarctica winter under their boat. They were
doing research on the penguin's population.

Running Shoes Are Cheaper Than Insulin

Post Office and Souvenir Shop

As you can see, the outpost is surrounded by penguins, and the penguins have the right of way. In the next photo, you'll see a young penguin getting regurgitated food from its parent. The white bird appears to be observing. This bird enjoys this same type of food. So it either waits for the food to fall on the ground or causes the baby penguin to miss food by nudging or distracting the penguin. Once the food is on the ground, neither penguin wants it. Thus, the bird has a free meal.

After dinner, about 60 people decided to sleep out under the stars. Yes, they took their sleeping bags and camped out on a small island...in the cold...in the snow. I decided to get a good night sleep before we begin crossing the Drake Passage.

BTW - Over 200 photos were taken of the penguins and whales. Thank goodness for digital photography. I would have run out of film.

The day ended with a beautiful sunset.

I had an interesting discussion with a non-runner. He had some interesting observations about this group of runners. For example, during the mealtime briefings, there's always excitement in the air. You can't help but get swept up in the excitement.

He compared it to going to sales, multi-level marketing, or a revival event. The only difference is that you're already "pumped up" by your previous accomplishments. Thus, we're a very highly, self-motivated group of individuals. It's hard to sit amongst this group without reconsidering or revising your own personal goals and/or priorities.

Goodnight.

Running Shoes Are Cheaper Than Insulin

Culerville Island & Fournier Bay, Antarctica, March 2

This is our last full day in Antarctica. We decided to spend it kayaking, visiting penguin colonies, and pursuing whales. It was also my last chance to take some memorable photos.

I can say that there are very few things in life that equate to being next to the world's largest animal without being afraid. The views were fantastic and it was a photographer's dream.

Yesterday, the whales seemed to stay along the surface. Today, in a different harbor, they were diving for food. This allowed us to get some very good "tail" shots. When they dived, it created a circle of still water.

Running Shoes Are Cheaper Than Insulin

The whales were magnificent and very graceful in their movements. These next two photos are meant to show the proportion of the surrounding mountains and glaciers with regards to the size of the kayaks. Some of these mountains are more than 3,000 feet.

Notice the people in the kayaks near the base of the above snow and rock formation. They appear to be specks.

Running Shoes Are Cheaper Than Insulin

An avalanche.

After visiting the wildlife, we went to an area that's known for its icebergs and snow-capped mountains—Fournier Bay.

Beginning this evening, we'll start crossing the Drake Passage. If we're fortunate, we'll have a relatively calm sea.

Goodnight!!!

Drake Passage Crossing, March 3 And 4

We had relatively calm seas for the 545-mile return crossing. The favorite phrase used by the tour guides is that we may have a "Drake Lake" (calm waters) or "Drake Quake" (rough seas). We've been very fortunate. The major question upon departing Antarctica was whether or not to wear the motion sickness patches. Based on the sightings at breakfast, most people decided to play it safe and wear their patch.

Most of our meal-time discussions focus on the Fin del Mundo Marathon and learning about other interesting marathons throughout the world.

Also, we saw a large group of about 30 whales. They were heading south. Although they were about one or two miles away, you could easily see their spouts shooting water in the air.

We were told that there will be a CD produced for us. It will contain the details of our tour and include our favorite personal photos. Thus, most people spent the crossing by downloading and editing photos for the CD. During a tour wrap-up session this evening, we previewed some of the photos. They were stunning.

As we approached South America, we were joined by some dolphins. They swam beside us for a while.

This evening, we're having dinner with the captain. Unfortunately, all of us forgot to pack our formal evening attire, so he had to overlook our clothes and enjoy the meal.

Running Shoes Are Cheaper Than Insulin

After the dinner, they gave us the CD-ROMs that contain additional information about the trip.

I have to finish packing. Our luggage has to be outside of our rooms for a 6:30 pickup. Most of us are staying for the Fin del Mundo Marathon on Tuesday.

Goodnight!!! I can't wait to sleep in a real bed and have my own shower!!!

Post-Trip Comments

I've decided that I want to return to Antarctica and campout overnight. Words cannot describe the feeling of being here. There was excitement from start to finish.

I'm feeling very comfortable with international travel and two-week vacations.

It's hard to really appreciate the problems that early explorers experienced until you "walk in their shoes." I couldn't imagine having my ship trapped in ice and having to live in Antarctica through two winters without losing a single man. Amazing!!!

Lessons Learned

- Whether running on the 3,600 steps during the Great Wall of China Marathon or the 17 percent angle Collin Glacier in Antarctica, it still takes a lot of small steps to achieve a goal.
- Don't stress out over things that you can't control, such as the weather. Just focus on the thing that you can control—you.

SOUTH AMERICA (ARGENTINA) - FIN DEL MUNDO MARATHON

Date: March 6, 2007
Marathon Number: 83
International Marathon Number: 6
Inspirational Song:
" A Psychoalphadiscobetabioaquadoloop" performed
by Parliament

Race Selection Process

The travel agency was able to convince the Fin Del Mundo Race Director to switch their marathon date to accommodate our docking. Thus, we were able to complete marathons on two continents in one trip. This saved both time and money. However, this meant running two marathons within eight days.

Travel Log

Land Ho!!! The Return To Ushuaia And The Weird Weather, March 5

Our ship finally arrived back to Ushuaia. We "parked" next to a huge ocean liner. During our trip to Antarctica, we were told that these ocean liners hold about 3000 people. When they take a cruise to Antarctica, for the most part, they stay on the ship. If they're lucky, they get to step on the continent for about 15 minutes in groups of 100 people.

We spent hours on excursions in and around the various bays and channels and untold time standing in "penguin poop." Someone described it as living ten days inside the pages of a National Geographic Magazine.

After we left the ship, we hit the main shopping strip in Ushuaia for food and last-minute souvenirs. During dinner, the conversation centered on the weather and what to wear during tomorrow's race. During the start of dinner, we could easily see the glacier and a beautiful picture of Ushuaia. Within a twenty-minute time span, we saw a blinding snowstorm come and go.

Running Shoes Are Cheaper Than Insulin

This little weather problem had occurred all day. As you can see, we couldn't see the city or the glacier. The snow was so thick that it caused the outdoor light to turn on. Do we wear singlets and shorts or tights and jackets? We were just happy that we didn't have to run up and down another glacier!!!!

Goodnight!!!

Fin Del Mundo Marathon, March 6

The morning started with a 7:00AM bus ride to the start of the Fin Del Mundo Marathon. Most of us decided to dress in layers. Thus, we could peel off our clothes if the weather became warm. We were told during dinner that Fox TV would be taping the marathon and interviewing runners.

Naturally, I posed with the mascots of the race.

An interesting little side note, I was told that beavers, foxes, and rabbits were not native to this area. They were introduced to be hunted for their fur. However, since they didn't have any natural enemies, their population exploded. During our bus ride, we probably saw over 50 rabbits.

The following photos are scenes from the race course.

Running Shoes Are Cheaper Than Insulin

While parts of the race were very beautiful, the section that passed near the airport was extremely windy. I felt sorry for anyone under 125 pounds. The wind was going to blow them away. One runner remarked that he was handed a cup of water at an aid station. Before he could put it to his lips, the wind blew the water completely out of his cup.

Running Shoes Are Cheaper Than Insulin

A fellow runner and I dragged our way through about 15 to 20 miles of the marathon when his wife appeared. There's nothing like having your spouse meet you on the race course and drag you to the finish line. She had finished the race earlier.

The last few miles of the race were spent talking about food. All I wanted was either a Snickers bar or orange/tangerine Jelly Belly Beans. After we finished, we walked a couple of blocks to the taxi stand.

As luck would have it, the taxi stand was right in front of a grocery store. Yes, I ran/limped in and bought five Snickers!!! I gave two to the husband and wife team, ate two on the spot, and saved one for a midnight snack. (I'll have it with my ham and cheese sandwich, which was smuggled from the bar.)

With this trip, I've completed my 82nd and 83rd marathons on my fifth and sixth continents. Africa is the only remaining continent in my quest. It's 11:30PM and I still have to pack for an 8AM departure. When I arrive in Dallas, I'll have a craving for IHOP pancakes (BIG HINT!!!!).

Goodnight!!!

Post-Marathon Events

While I felt a "rush" after completing two marathons in eight days on two continents, I still had to face the reality of returning to work and deciding whether to run the Safaricom Lewa Marathon in Kenya.

It was great seeing my girlfriend at the airport. My attention turned to preparing for the ING Georgia and the Rite-Aid Cleveland Marathons in March and April, respectively.

Lessons Learned

- You appreciate the most simple pleasures, such as a Snickers and hot shower, after tough marathons.
- You don't worry about the things you can't control, such as the weather. You only focus on what you can control, such your race clothing.

AFRICA (KENYA) - SAFARICOM LEWA MARATHON

Date: June 23, 2007
Marathon Number: 7
International Marathon Number: 7
Inspirational Song: "Chocolate City" performed by Parliament

Race Selection Process

While in Ushuaia, my friends kept talking to me about running with them in Kenya's Safaricom Marathon. The tour was again through Marathon Tours and Travel. If we completed it, it would be the final jewel in our seven-continent quest. It would be fitting for Africa to be my last race.

During the Antarctica tour, the race director told me that only two other Blacks had completed the Antarctica Marathon. He also said that no Blacks had completed marathons on all seven continents, to the best of his knowledge.

I had considered running the Two Oceans or the Johannesburg Marathons in South Africa. However, I had to evaluate my financial situation and vacation time closely.

Over the next couple of weeks, my girlfriend and I discussed the Safaricom Marathon and the possibility of being the first Black to complete the goal. I found myself reflecting back on my first day in the silk shop in China. The opportunity to purchase the silk comforter may never come again. I had to trust my instinct.

Being the first in the world is a once-in-a-lifetime opportunity. After checking my credit card balances, budget, and savings accounts, I registered for the trip. My girlfriend encouraged me to follow my dreams. I felt that I could always make more money.

I also realized that despite the possibility of being the first Black in the world to accomplish this feat, I could not let my employer know about my plans. Most employers would jump at the opportunity for the free publicity.

Running Shoes Are Cheaper Than Insulin

Although they supported an employee who climbed Mt. Everest, they discouraged me from running international marathons. Even at my own expense and on my own time. More than 500 people climbed Mt. Everest in 2007 alone. However, fewer than 225 people in the world had ever run marathons on all seven continents.

For this reason, I embarked on this trip without any fanfare. Only my girlfriend and closest relatives were aware of my pursuit to make history. My employer didn't even know where I was going for vacation.

Travel Log

Monday, June 16, 2007, 12:45 AM - Nairobi, Kenya (Monday, 4:45 PM Central Time)

Happy Father's Day!!! My morning started in Amsterdam. The lines at the airport were long for the KLM flight to Nairobi. However, once I made my way to the flight's gate, I started to see some familiar faces from the Great Wall of China and Antarctica tours. Naturally, the conversations focused on other marathons. The KLM flight was OK. I started watching the 1978 Parliament/Funkadelic Concert DVD and when the DVDs finished, I continued reading Enders Game.

The flight touched down around 7:15PM. We had a long wait at the airport for our luggage. It was dark outside and we didn't see very much. We arrived at the Norfolk Hotel in Nairobi around 9:45PM. Since the restaurant closed at 10, we went straight to dinner.

Yes, I wore the same fisherman's vest from the Australia, China, Antarctica, and Argentina Marathons. I've decided to officially retire it after the completion of this race. And yes, I'm a beer I'm drinking with my pizza. It's a local brand called Tusker. I rarely drink because I'm usually driving. However, since I won't be behind the wheel for a couple of weeks, I can have a few brews.

After dinner, I went to my room, which is more like a suite with a sitting room. I discovered that I brought every electrical outlet converter, except the one I needed. Fortunately, the hotel had one. So, I charged my DVD battery packs and worked on the website. Unfortunately, I may not get to upload anything until I get to Paris.

Monday, June 18 - Aberdare National Park (The Ark)

I woke up a 7:45AM for our 9AM departure to Aberdare National Park. So, my breakfast consisted of Rice Krispy Treats, a Fig Newton, pound cake, and water. I ran into some of my "tour mates" from Texas. We ran the Great Wall of China, Antarctica, and Fin Del Mundo (Argentina) Marathons together. The Safaricom Marathon will be our seventh continent.

On our way to Aberdare, we stopped at the African Curio Shop. I felt like I was back in China. We had to bargain for everything.

Running Shoes Are Cheaper Than Insulin

On our way, we saw a Starbucks. Unfortunately, it wasn't for coffee drinkers.

During lunch, we had a mini Great Wall Marathon reunion. We were told about the challenges during this race. The race was held at a high altitude, mostly in the sun, and with steep hills. It would be cool in the morning and warm after one-and-a-half hours into the race.

You had to be careful of over hydration, dehydration, and heat stroke. And we had to watch out for the animals. It was their territory and they roam freely throughout the park. We arrived at the Ark in Aberdare National Park around 5:30PM.

The Ark is located near the animals' watering hole. There's an outdoor deck and an enclosed patio for us to watch the animals. We were really excited to see an elephant. It was licking the salt off of the ground. All of the sudden, a baby elephant and its mother came running from around the corner.

Running Shoes Are Cheaper Than Insulin

During dinner, we were joined by a retired couple whom we also met in China. The dinner was fantastic.

After dinner, we went to the patio for more animal watching. We saw several elephants, water buffalos with a calf, lots of bugs, and other animals.

It's been a long day and a very late night. Goodnight.

Tuesday, June 19, Mt. Kenya Safari Club on the Equator (Zero Degrees Latitude) at 7000 Feet Altitude

I awoke around 4:30 this morning to a loud roar. I put on some clothes and went to the inside patio observation deck. An elephant, water buffalo, impalas, birds, and hyenas were at the water hole. After taking some more photos, I returned to bed.

We had a great breakfast. I must admit, I've been thoroughly impressed with the food. I think that this may be the first time that I'll get to the marathon's starting line heavier than I had planned. After breakfast, we boarded the buses to the Mt. Kenya Safari Club (MKSC). This is about a two-hour drive from the Ark. Along the way out of the reservation, we ran into impalas, wart hogs, giraffes, zebras, and a few bucks.

Running Shoes Are Cheaper Than Insulin

During our bus rides, we noticed national police road stops. They lay material on the group to blow out tires. We understand that they're attempting to stop the flow of terrorists into their country.

On our way, we stopped at the Equator "Shopping Mall" for photos and more souvenirs. Some of the stalls were named after US locations. Since we live in Texas, we stopped in the Texas and Dallas stalls. Bargaining was hot and fast.

However, we learned that on our next trip, we should bring American clothes and women's fashion magazines to trade. After purchasing the globe in China, I found myself drawn to items with the world map. It would be a fitting reward for finishing the seventh continent.

The Texas and Dallas Shops.

Running Shoes Are Cheaper Than Insulin

We finally arrived at the Mt. Kenya Safari Club for lunch.
We'll stay here for two nights.

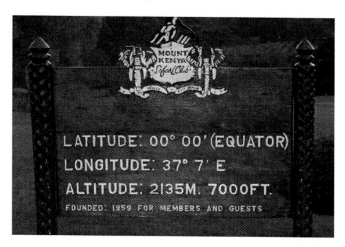

It took our breath away. someone had a magazine that
rated the top hotels and resorts in the world by continent.
This place was ranked third in Africa. It's "laid out." The
bungalows are great.

During lunch, I learned that two of the women from the Antarctica Marathon may be in the Guinness Book of World Records. One climbed Mt. Everest last month. She became the first woman to run a marathon on all seven continents AND climb the highest peak on all seven. The other one completed a marathon on all seven continents in the shortest time period. It was her second time to complete the seven AND she added the North Pole Marathon to her list. (I feel totally sane after hearing about them.)

After lunch and a brief rest, we went for a short run. As the group (about 20 people) approached the gate, the guard looked stunned. And he should have been, based on the sign below.

However, after he took a body count, he opened the gate and let us run through the game reserve. We really felt the impact of running at 7,000 feet. I was heaving during and after the run. I felt like someone was pounding on my chest.

After about 3 miles, I felt like I had finished a marathon!!! It's no wonder that Kenyans are the best in distance running. Fortunately, the actual race will be at another location. Its altitude is between 5,200 and 5,800 feet.

I felt out of breath while walking up the hill to dinner. The food was great. This has led to an unusual problem. I packed some "insurance" food for the trip: ten Ramen Noodle Soup Cups. If the local meals weren't sufficient, I at least would have one "reliable" meal a day. As I emptied food from this suit case, I would use it for the souvenirs.

Unfortunately (or fortunately), I haven't had to use the food. So, now I have an over-packing problem. During dinner, we discussed my dilemma I. Someone recommended that I use the food to barter with at our next stop!!! I also realized that I'd be attending a wedding when I return. So, I've decided to get the gifts in Kenya and France.

The altitude run today has made me feel wiped out. Also, I've averaged about five hours sleep for the past few nights. Tonight, I'm hoping to get a full eight-hours sleep. I need it.

Goodnight.

Wednesday, June 20 - Mt. Kenya Safari Club, Nature Walk With The Armed Guards

Last night was very rough. I awoke at 3:00 with a sore throat. I was afraid that I may have caught the flu from another runner. Since it was cold, I had the fireplace lit. I think the ash in the air triggered the reaction. After about an hour, I was able to return to sleep.

We assembled at 8:00 for a three-hour nature hike through the game reserve. Our guide, Simon, informed us that we would be accompanied by armed guards since the animals roamed freely. Also, our compound is protected by an electric fence. Once we step outside of the fence, anything could happen. It's no wonder the guard looked surprised yesterday.

Running Shoes Are Cheaper Than Insulin

About 20 people went on the hike. Every time we walked up a hill, we were reminded about the altitude. I wanted to slow down and was breathing heavily. Our first stop was the old Mawingo Airstrip. We were joined by three armed park rangers. Since we had so many people, we split into two groups.

One of the first things we came across was a zebra's "after birth" on the old airstrip. After about an hour of walking, we saw the zebra herd in the distance.

After about 45 minutes, we met the other group, took a break, and posed for photos.

Running Shoes Are Cheaper Than Insulin

On our way back to the airstrip, we didn't see very much. However, the airstrip was abuzz with activity. We saw a herd crossing the airstrip. They were followed closely by a couple of hyenas. After that herd passed, a family of wart hogs decided to go across. After we were back on the property, we crossed a stream on a makeshift bridge.

After lunch, I learned that their Internet connection worked!!!!! So I spent some time by the pool and uploaded the photos. When I returned to my bungalow, the horses were grazing in the pasture.

Around 3:00, the Texas tour mates and I went to the Mt. Kenya Animal Orphanage. The most interesting animal was a cross between a female zebra and male horse.

I returned to my bungalow for the evening. I realized that 7:30 dinners may have had an impact on my ability to sleep. So, this evening, I decided to have some of the soup that I brought. Also, as luck would have it, it started raining. Thanks to the souvenirs, I now have to repack my

Running Shoes Are Cheaper Than Insulin

luggage before tomorrow morning's departure to the Lewa Wildlife Sanctuary. My objective is to be asleep by 10.

Thursday, June 21 - Lewa Wildlife Sanctuary, Kenya

I'm still feeling under the weather. My sinuses are killing me from the fireplace on Tuesday night. At least I was able to get eight hours of sleep. We departed Mt. Kenya around 11AM, instead of 10AM. This gave me extra time to upload the previous day's activities.

We arrived at the Lewa Wildlife Sanctuary about two hours later. This is where the real adventure begins. They transferred our luggage to trucks while we boarded open-top Land Rovers. I can't begin to describe what we witnessed. It's one thing to see giraffes, elephants, zebras, and ostriches in zoos. It's another thing to see them in their natural habitats. Also, seeing packs of the animals, instead of just one or two, is equally exciting.

Note: These are two different zebras. The top one has thin stripes and none on its belly. The bottom one has wider stripes with stripes on its belly.

Running Shoes Are Cheaper Than Insulin

After our arrival at camp, we split into two groups and had lunch. Lunch consisted of fish and fries. Since the fish wasn't shaped like a McDonald's fish, I just had fries. :-)

I'm happy that I was a camper while growing up. This experience makes you appreciate the simple pleasures of city living.

My new tent home.

They had named our tents. Mine is macaranga. This is a tropical tree that's native to Africa.

Running Shoes Are Cheaper Than Insulin

The shower stall (left) and outhouse (right).

The Mess Tent & View

I picked up my race number and listened to the pre-race report. This marathon is rated as one of the ten toughest in the world. This is due to the heat, dryness, and altitude. However, some of the best runners in the world will be

Running Shoes Are Cheaper Than Insulin

here. However, since most of them are Kenyan anyway, this will be "a walk in the park" for them.

The race director informed us that there are aid stations about every 2K. Also, we must be at the 20K (12.5-mile) point within three hours, twenty minutes. This is my goal. He also said that we should expect to run this race about one to two minutes a mile slower than we normally run. The two-loop course would be hilly.

The race t-shirts are great. They'll definitely stand out since they have zebra stripes on them. There would be airplanes and helicopters in the air during the race to "encourage" the animals to stay away from the road.

Around 5:30, we went for a pre-dinner safari drive. The temperature nose-dived and I should have worn a long-sleeve jacket. While we saw many of the same animals, we had an interesting encounter with a family of elephants.

They were by the side of the road grazing. The mother decided to take the three babies across the road to the creek. However, they stopped on the road. The mother decided to protect her children and we had a face-off. Naturally, they won.

Dinner was great. I'm going to try to wake up at 6AM for the 6:30 game drive.

Goodnight.

Running Shoes Are Cheaper Than Insulin

Friday, June 22 - Lewa Wildlife Sanctuary, Kenya

I actually had a good night's sleep thanks to the Clarion-D. While the cot looks bad, it felt better than the bed at Mt. Kenya. However, it was quite an adventure going to the toilet tent around 4AM. I had to get dressed and put on my boots to walk through the tall grass.

We rose around 6AM for a 6:30 nature drive. As usual, the scenery and animals were great. However, we saw rhinos, zebras, and cheetahs on the marathon course.

These three cheetahs are brothers. They hunt together very well as a team and are very protective of their territory. Yes, they're walking on the race course. Notice the red directional arrow.

Running Shoes Are Cheaper Than Insulin

On our way back to camp, we ran into the zebra "bachelor's club" and a bar fight scene. There's a herd of young male zebras. These guys were practicing their fighting techniques.

It's 8:30PM and I'm preparing to go to bed. I have to awake at 4:45AM to catch the bus. The main discussions centered on race day and the related pre-race rituals. I carefully laid out my running clothes, pinned on my race number, mixed Gatorade, and organized my "Batman utility belt" with my camera and orange jelly beans.

Most people are concerned about the bad combination of warm weather and high altitude. We're always reminded about the lady who died, the man who was evacuated out, and the large number of runners who have required post-race medical attention.

If you happen to have a large body type and will be on the course for a long time period, you may be in serious trouble. Also, based on what we've seen of the course, it's mostly in the sun. Unfortunately, this accurately describes me!!! However, I have a few things on my side:

1. I live and train in the heat.
2. I've run two recent marathons (Salt Lake City and Albuquerque) at high altitudes and didn't have any problems.
3. I've run 86 marathons in all types of weather and have a lot of experience to draw from.
4. I've overridden my ego and quit a marathon in 1994. (There will always be other marathons.)
5. I've overridden my ego and cut short training runs due to the heat. (There will always be better days to train.)

I hope all of this overrides the obstacles. My priorities for this race are simple:

- To live.
- To live to run another day.
- To finish the race.
- To complete the first 20K (12.5 miles) in under 3 hours, 20 minutes. This is the cutoff time.
- To run in the shade as much as possible, even in the shade of another runner.

If I keep these things in mind and stay focused, I should be alright. (The cheetah may run fast, but the turtle lives longer.)

Goodnight.

Saturday, June23 - Safaricom Marathon Race Day

We were awakened at 4:30AM to prep for the race and grab a bite to eat. I ate the cup of noodles since it's easily digestible and contains carbs and salt. We loaded into the Land Rovers at 5:30 for the ride to the race.

Running Shoes Are Cheaper Than Insulin

It occurred to me that this is the first race where I won't be in the minority. The weather was cool and cloudy. Since there wasn't very much shade on the course, we hoped the sun stayed hidden.

Everywhere we looked, we saw children. People were running in every type of shoe imaginable. We saw a herd of zebras running across the road. Airplanes and helicopters buzzed overhead to keep the more dangerous animals away.

Yes...That's a special National Black Marathoners' Association running jersey made especially for the race. It will be retired to a shadow box with the trip's mementos.

This was not your typical Boston, Chicago, or NYC Marathon. After the race started, I didn't recall seeing any buildings. The largest crowd, not counting the aid station workers, was about 40 people during the first lap. It was about five people during the second lap. However, the landscape and scenery were beautiful. Plus, the bugs didn't bother me.

The weather was perfect. The sun stayed behind the clouds and kept the temperature cool. I didn't even have to wear my hat during the race. A slight breeze also helped. We followed our plan of drinking plenty of electrolytes (and orange jelly beans) during the race.

I ran most of the way with an Australian. We kept within sight of another runner. We used photo-taking, Vaseline-rubbing, and rocks-in-shoes opportunities to take breaks. The company was very well appreciated. (I think that we felt that four or six eyes looking out for animals was much better than two eyes.)

Running Shoes Are Cheaper Than Insulin

A warning sign that two hills are ahead.

Running Shoes Are Cheaper Than Insulin

After I crossed the finish line, I learned that one of my Texas tour mates won her age group. Since I carried cash in my "Batman utility belt," I decided to get Paul Tergat's book. He's the Kenyan who holds the world's best marathon time of 2:04:55. Since he was at the race, he autographed a copy for me. The post-race goodie bag was also nice.

Several of us decided to wait for the final Texan to finish the race. Since the airlines had lost her luggage, she needed all the support she could get during the trip.

Today, we each joined the Seven Continents Club by completing a marathon on all seven continents. I've decided that I'd like to return to this marathon again. The experience was great.

Take care.

Post-Marathon Events

After the Kenyan marathon, I spent a week in Paris consolidating and writing two books about my global running and business experiences.

I returned to work from my scheduled vacation on July 2— my birthday. I was immediately laid off. What a birthday present!!! It's said, "When one door closes, bigger and better doors open." On the bright side, since I had been on vacation for two weeks, I didn't feel like my not-going-to-work habit was disrupted!!!

My girlfriend's daughter was getting married a few days later on 07/07/07. Since I had some "spare" time, I was immediately drafted in being their chauffer, table cloth ironer, wedding program designer and printer, and freelance photographer. It was fun and a great distraction. I jokingly said I could add these tasks to my resume and work for a wedding coordinator.

On the evening of the wedding, there was a Seven Continents celebration party. My girlfriend and I went from the wedding reception to the party and back to the post-wedding party. We must have driven over a hundred miles that afternoon and evening.

On July 17, a door opened. Thom Gilligan of Marathon Tours and Travel distributed the following press release.

FOR IMMEDIATE RELEASE

First Black Runner Finishes Seven Marathons on Seven Continents
Global Trail Blazer Heads Up National Black Marathoners' Association

BOSTON (July 17, 2007) – Tony Reed, the executive director and co-founder of the National Black Marathoners' Association (NBMA), has become the first Black runner to finish a marathon on all seven continents, announced Marathon Tours and Travel, a travel agency for marathon runners and organizer of the Seven Continents Club.

The Dallas-area runner has completed 26.2-mile jaunts in locales as far as flung the Great Wall of China, as icy as Antarctica and as precarious as an African game park. A finisher of over 87 marathons, Reed wrapped up his seven-on-seven goal at the Safaricom Lewa Marathon in Kenya on June 23, 2007.

"Tony's spirit of adventure and love of the sport of running will no doubt motivate and inspire others in his community to pursue a healthy and active lifestyle," said Thom Gilligan, founder of Marathon Tours and Travel and its Seven Continents Club, a travel club for runners that offers special recognition for members who have completed seven marathons or seven half marathons on all seven continents.

Reed's international finishes include: the Cowtown Marathon (Ft. Worth, TX); Tailwinds Marathon (Copenhagen, Denmark); Gold Coast Marathon (Australia); Great Wall of China Marathon; Antarctic Marathon; Fin Del Mundo Marathon (Ushuaia, Argentina) and the Safaricom Lewa Marathon in Kenya.

Reed, who grew up in a St. Louis housing project, co-founded the National Black Marathoners' Association in 2004. The non-profit organization's mission is to encourage Black Americans to pursue a healthy lifestyle through running and to raise awareness of the health risks that are more prevalent among Blacks. The 500-member organization also awards college scholarships to high school distance runners.

"I was diagnosed with increased glucose levels but have been able to avoid full-blown diabetes by maintaining a healthy diet and by exercising," said Reed, who has a family history of the disease.

"I also want to set an example and inspire other Blacks to set and reach goals," said Reed, a speaker, an information technology consultant, and CPA who holds two masters and two bachelors degrees. The NBMA estimates that African Americans only make up one to two percent of all US marathoners.

Reflecting on his African continental finale, Reed said "The Safaricom Marathon was the first race I have ever been in where I did not feel like a minority."

For more information on Marathon Tours and Travel and the Seven Continents Club, please visit www.marathontours.com or call (617) 242-7845. For more information on the NBMA, visit www.BlackMarathoners.org.

Running Shoes Are Cheaper Than Insulin

A few days later, another door opened. Runner's World asked me to write an article about my experience in their website's First Person Blog section.

RunnersWorld.com's First Person Blog – July 17, 2007

Tony Reed: How I Became the First Black Runner to Complete Marathons on All Seven Continents

By Tony Reed

On the eve of Kenya's Safaricom Lewa Marathon, I was a nervous wreck. This race would be the final jewel in my quest to run a marathon on all seven continents (7C). As the Co-Founder and Executive Director of the National Black Marathoners' Association (NBMA), I felt that it was fitting for Africa to be the grand finale. Hundreds of people were awaiting the results of the race. I was also nervous because I may be the first Black in the world to accomplish the 7C feat. (Several groups are helping me confirm this.)

Since my first marathon in 1982, I've counted the number of Blacks in all the races I entered. Occasionally, I was the only one. Anytime there were more than 10 Blacks, I felt happy. Thus, running in a predominately Black marathon would be very different.

As the only Black in races, or one of few, I've felt that my failure to finish would leave a negative impression about American Blacks and the discipline to complete distance races. I especially felt this pressure during Antarctica's Last Marathon in February. I was the lone Black runner on the "white continent." I don't think my friends would have let me live it down, if I had quit the race.

In Kenya, as I lay in my tent the night before the Safaricom Lewa Marathon, I thought about the warnings from the pre-race meeting. We faced a dangerous mixture of high altitude (5,200 ft.), dry air, and heat. Hyponatremia, the dilution of sodium by over-hydrating with water, was a risk before and during the race. Fortunately, I've trained in the Texas heat for 30 years. And I ran the New Mexico (5,800 ft.) and Salt Lake City (4,800 ft.) Marathons without any problems. Thus, I thought about the new, more challenging obstacles: wild animal attacks.

The day before the race, we saw three cheetahs, two rhinos, and a zebra herd on the marathon course. The animals would be roaming freely during the race. After all, it was their home and we runners were just visitors. As the cheetahs walked by the race marker, I asked our guide, "How often do they eat?" He replied, "They're excellent hunters and work as a team to easily bring down a zebra. It would provide enough food for about three days."

I hoped that there would be one less zebra before tomorrow's race. But I realized that I couldn't control the weather or the wild animals, so I stopped worrying about them. Instead, I focused on what I could control: me. Somehow, I managed to fall asleep.

On race day, I got on my running groove while listening to Parliament/Funkadelic's Cosmic Slop and Chocolate City. During the ride to the starting area, I didn't see any animals. But I did notice the airplanes. At the starting line, I marveled at being surrounded by hundreds of Black runners. It didn't matter that I didn't speak their language. I felt good just being there. It was like being at my first family reunion. I didn't know anyone, but the closeness was in the air. I saw groups of school children in their team colors straining behind the tape to watch us start. They were also awaiting the start of their own race.

When the race started, I felt like the entire NBMA was running vicariously with me. We had just finished another successful gathering at the May, 2007 Rite-Aid Cleveland Marathon. The veteran runners noted that I may be the first Black marathoner to complete the seven continents goal. About 200 other runners had achieved it before me.

Midway up a long curving the hill, my eyes began to tear up. As I looked in front and behind me, I saw a long stream of Black runners. In 25 years of running 86 marathons and 150 races, I had never seen this many Blacks in a distance race. Unforgettable.

After the first loop, hundreds of half marathoners turned off towards their finish line. Suddenly, we marathoners were alone. After participating in marathons with thousands of runners and cheering spectators, skyscrapers, and TV helicopters, the solitude (with the exception of an occasional buzz) was a welcome relief. This is what long distance running is all about--enjoying nature in all its beauty.

The runners and crowds were transformed into waves of blowing grasses. The skyscrapers became majestic mountains. And the TV helicopters were replaced by the prop planes. They "buzzed" the wild animals to keep them away from the course. Around 40K, I reached the safety of the compound's fenced area. I decided to finish the marathon alone.

I wanted to savor the moment and reflect on the challenges I had overcome to reach this pinnacle. Who would have imagined that a Black, non-athletic, inner city kid from St. Louis would have run 87 marathons in 25 States and seven continents, including Antarctica?

This went against the odds, but then, so have so many things in my life. I gathered myself together and crossed the finish line as (possibly) the first Black in the world to join the exclusive Seven Continents Club. I topped off my adventure by having Kenya's Paul Tergat, the marathon world record holder, to autograph a copy of his biography, "Paul Tergat – Running to the Limit."

Doors continued to open.

In August, I was contacted by TheFinalSprint.com to be interviewed about my experiences. I was interviewed by Adam Jacobs and Don Kern. Don and I met in the locker room at New Hampshire Marathon on September 30, 2006. We later reconnected at the Antarctica Marathon in February, 2007. It was a small world.

The interview was released as a podcast and I was selected to be their Success Story of the month. This award is given "to individuals, who have overcome tremendous obstacles, changed their own lives and/or the lives of others through running, sports or fitness." This was a real honor.

Another door opened in September. I received an email from Runner's World. They wanted to write an article for their hardcopy publication about my accomplishment and the National Black Marathoners' Association. This was a runner's dream. It's the equivalent of having a photo spread in National Geographic. The article appeared in their February 2008 edition.

MEMORABLE US MARATHONS

Wills Point, TX – Daybreak Marathon (04/30/1983)

Marathon Number: 4

One of my training partners, Paul, and I decided to run the Daybreak Marathon in Wills Point, TX. This small town is about 50 miles east of Dallas. Due to the Texas heat, the race started at 5:30 in the morning. This was roughly 30 minutes before daybreak.

Since Paul and I were "experienced" marathoners, we knew to arrive about an hour before the race. We needed to pick up our race packets, use the restrooms, and stretch. We arrived to a darkened town around 4:30 and pulled up in front of a building.

We didn't see any "signs of life." We checked the map and re-read the instructions. We were at the right location. However, there wasn't any of the pre-race hoopla that we had seen at previous events.

After about ten minutes, a police car pulls up beside us and rolls down his window. He said, "Do you realize that you're parked in front of the town's bank?" We explained that we must be lost. A race is supposed to start here in less than an hour. Just then, a man pulls up in a pickup truck. It's the race director.

He held the registration and packet pickup from his flatbed. The race directions were simple. Run to the corner. Turn right at the stop sign. Keep running until we tell you to turn around and come back.

The race started and it was still dark. We heard roosters crowing, but didn't see anything. As the sun peeked out, we saw the most beautiful countryside. It was breathtaking. The aid stations were manned by Boy Scouts.

During the race, I kept hearing buzzing sounds. I noticed that bees were zipping back and forth across the country road. The last thing that I needed was to be strung by one. Occasionally, one would fly into me and begin chasing me. I found myself doing "speed work" in the final few miles of the race.

We finished the race by crossing the finish line on Main Street during a fair. I began to think that we were the entertainment for the morning. After the race, we didn't receive finisher medals, race results, or t-shirts, just the satisfaction of knowing that you participated.

Denton, TX - North Texas State University (now University of North Texas) Marathon (10/22/1983)

Marathon Number: 5

In 1982, I participated in the 12th Annual NTSU Marathon. The course was designed as a double loop that started and finished in the football stadium parking lot.

Since I enjoy the solitude during long runs, I registered for the race and wanted to use it as a long training run. My plan was to run the first 20 miles and take it very easy over the last 6.2 miles.

The weather wasn't very cooperative. It was warm and humid. It rained so hard before the race that a dry creek bed had become a fast-moving stream. The race organizers placed old tires in the creek for the runners to make our way across.

After the first few miles, I didn't see another runner until around 18 miles. I passed him while he was walking. My finishing time was a respectable 3:53:24. I changed clothes and went home.

A few days later, my wife called me at work. She said that the race director had called me at home. He said that I had forgotten to pick up my first place age group trophy!!! I was shocked. It had to be a joke or misunderstanding.

I called the university and they confirmed everything. I dropped everything at work and drove to get the trophy. After reviewing the race results, I realized that the first-place finisher, Richard Weber, was in my age group; 20 to 29 years old.

My overall place was 24th out of 30. However, the last six finishers included everyone in my age group. Since Richard received the first place overall trophy, the race organizers didn't award more than one trophy to a runner. Thus, Richard couldn't receive the first place age group trophy. That went to me. The last five runners received age group trophies!!!

After this experience, I learned that when you achieve a goal, there may be other unforeseen rewards awaiting you.

The 131-Mile Texas Marathon Challenge (11/07/1999 through 02/26/2000)

Marathon Numbers: 34 through 38

Between 1982 and 1998, I averaged running two marathons a year. They were usually the Dallas White Rock Marathon in December and Ft. Worth's Cowtown Marathon in February. I had run them thirteen and fourteen times, respectively.

An article appeared in a regional running magazine about the Texas Marathon Challenge (TMC). It involved running the five largest marathons (131 miles) in Texas in only four months. They had to be completed before the official course closure time. They were:

Nov. 7, 1999	San Antonio Marathon
Dec. 5, 1999	Dallas White Rock Marathon
Jan. 16, 2000	Houston Marathon
Feb. 20, 2000	Austin Marathon
Feb. 26, 2000	Ft. Worth's Cowtown Marathon

The last two marathons were six days apart. The TMC went against most of the prevailing knowledge about marathons. It was that you only ran one or two marathons a year. Anything else was too taxing on the body and you couldn't properly recover.

However, I was looking for something different and this seemed to fit the bill. It also gave my family an opportunity to see the cities. The real challenge was running Cowtown only six days after the Austin Marathon.

Many of the participants purchased TMC singlets. They had the five marathons listed on the back. Next to each name was a checkbox. You filled it in as you completed the race.

Over the course of the races, the runners developed a bond. By the time we reached Cowtown, all I wanted to do was finish. I had run my best time at the White Rock Marathon and the slowest one at Cowtown. However, I ran even splits at Cowtown. Eighty-seven runners completed the challenge.

This event made me realize that I physically run more than two marathons a year. Between 2003 and 2007, I completed forty-three marathons, an average of about eleven marathons a year.

Lubbock, TX - Walk Of Fame Marathon (09/03/2000)

Marathon Number: 40

On Labor Day 2000, we were lining up for the start of Lubbock's Walk of Fame Marathon. The marathon honored Billy Holiday, their hometown music legend. Beads of sweat were already rolling down my forehead and the race had not even started. It was a warm morning and it was going to get a lot worse.

I didn't care about my finishing time. I just wanted to finish alive. It was so hot that an unchained, barking dog refused to venture from the shade to chase us. During the race, my main focus was to stay hydrated. The runners turned into shufflers. We looked like the walking wounded as the heat index and temperatures felt like they were over 100. I had to resort to what I call a "sun run." Using this strategy, I always walked in the shade and ran in the sun. I also took my hat off in the shade to cool my head and put it back on in the sun.

I drank at every aid station. I put ice cubes under my hat. I imagined that the cool water from the melting ice was a portable air conditioner. Unfortunately, despite well-stocked aid stations, I didn't drink enough to ward off heat cramps. As I was stepping off a curb, I pointed my toes downward to touch the street. At that very moment, the cramp started in my toes and progressed to my thigh. I was in real pain. I managed to limp the last mile to the finish. This was the only race that I didn't run across the finish line. I had just established my new "personal worst" marathon time. A lady frantically asked me if I had seen her husband on the course. It was his first marathon. When I saw him, he looked so bad that he made me look good. I had offered him advice on how to stay cool during the race.

From this day forth, my objective will be to finish marathons before this horrible time. It was more than two hours slower than my personal best time. I collapsed in the shade and a volunteer brought fluids. After a few minutes, they called my name. I had won third place in my weight division!!! I staggered to the stage to get my medal. I earned it. It had become a race of attrition. When I returned to my hotel room, I sat in the bath tub under a cold water shower.

The next day, I returned home as the proud, but tired, medal winner. A few days later, a package arrived at my home. There was another medal inside. Evidently, I had also placed third in my age group!!! Not bad for my slowest marathon time to date.

Spirit of St. Louis Marathon (04/04/2004)

Marathon Number: 56

This was first opportunity to run a marathon in my hometown, St. Louis, since I had left in 1978. And it was the first time that my father, his wife, and my sister, Tracy, had the opportunity to see me run.

Unbeknownst to me, the course went by my old university, former employer locations, and my first apartments. When the course went by the public housing where we briefly resided, some of the children decided to join me for a run.

It had me thinking about how far we had come in those forty years. It also had me thinking about the lives and dreams of those children. I wondered what impact it would have if race courses were routed through inner-city neighborhoods.

It would give the children an opportunity to see us and dream about joining us one day. We could serve as an example for adults who felt that their athletic accomplishments had to end when they graduated from high school or college.

If the adults and children were more physically active, we may be able to reduce the incidents of diabetes, heart disease, stroke, obesity, and other "diseases of inactivity." This idea became one of the missions of the National Black Marathoners' Association (NBMA).

Twelve Marathons In Twelve Months Plus An Ultra-Marathon (11/20/2004 through 10/08/2005)

Marathon Numbers: 60 through 71

There's something about approaching 50 years old and being a marathoner that made me reflect on some of the goals that I had "put on the back shelf." Since completing my first Texas Marathon Challenge in 2000, I always wanted to run twelve marathons in twelve months.

At the same time, I had several other goals that I could work towards achieving during those twelve months. They included:

- Completing either a 50K (31-miler) or 50-miler while 50 years old.
- Running marathons in all 50 states.
- Running marathons on all seven continents.

So, I decided to run the marathons and an ultra-marathon in different states and/or countries. The goal was completed on October 8, 2005. The races (and states) included:

- Oklahoma Marathon (OK)
- Orange County Marathon (CA)
- Las Vegas Marathon (NV)
- Mercedes/Birmingham (AL)
- Little Rock (AR)
- Eisenhower (KS)
- Flying Pig (Cincinnati, OH)
- Keybank Vermont (VT)
- Gold Coast Airport (Australia)
- Iowa Trails 50K (IA)
- Lewis & Clark (MO)
- Hartford United Tech (CT)

Each marathon was in a different state or country. The Australia's Gold Coast Marathon was on my 50th birthday, 07/02. My next race was the Iowa Trails 50K. This consisted of running seven times around a loop in a wooded area. As I crossed the finish line, the race official remarked that if I had been a little bit faster, I would have

finished in less than seven hours. My finishing time was
07:02, my birthday.

The NBMA Beginnings (2001 through 2007)

In July 2001, I was giving a presentation about goal setting
at the National Black Data Processing Association's
Annual Conference in Chicago. I mentioned my goal of
finishing 50 marathons before turning 50 years old. I had
completed 47 marathons at the time. Charlotte Simmons
was in the audience.

During the reception that followed, Charlotte introduced me
to a group of runners. She was the President of the South
Fulton Running Partners (SFRP), an Atlanta area Black
running club. They discussed the possibility of joining me
for my 50th marathon. We exchanged email addresses and
promised to stay in touch.

During the next couple of years, I kept the group apprised
of my progress as I approached the 50th race. I selected
the Dallas Trails Marathon as the location of the event. It
was on March 23, 2003.

There were usually less than 150 marathoners. Most of
them were local runners. The course was fast and flat. It
included my favorite running path, which encircled White
Rock Lake and proceeded to north Dallas.

On March 20, 2003, Operation Iraqi Freedom started and
the coalition forces invaded Iraq. The same day, the
Washington, DC, Marathon was cancelled for security
reasons. It was also scheduled for March 23. Over 7,000
registered runners had to make other plans.

Members of the SFRP decided to join Charlotte at the Dallas Trails Marathon. Since I was usually the only Black in the race, this sudden influx of Black runners was unusual. When the race was over, most of these runners, including me, had won age group or weight division trophies.

We had such a good time that we began to discuss how much fun it would be to gather at a different marathon annually. This later became one of the missions for the NBMA.

In December 2004, after emails and phone calls, the National Black Marathoners' Association was incorporated in Texas as a not-for-profit organization and our initial website was created. Our threefold mission is to:

- Encourage Black Americans and others to pursue a healthy lifestyle through long-distance running and walking.
- Serve as a vehicle for Black American distance runners across the nation to meet in mass at a single marathon.
- Provide scholarships to deserving high school boy-and-girl distance runners.

Various running publications supported the organization by announcing our formation. They later announced the location of our first mass gathering at the 2005 Lewis & Clark Marathon and Half Marathon in St. Charles, MO. We also gathered at the New Jersey and Rite-Aid Cleveland Marathons in 2006 and 2007, respectively.

About a dozen runners joined us in 2005. By 2007, over 150 people participated in Cleveland.

OTHER FACTS

91 Marathons Completed As Of 2007

Fastest Marathon Time
Age: 29
Date: December 2, 1984
Race: Dallas White Rock Marathon
Time: 3:36:45

Slowest Marathon Time
Age: 50
Date: May 20, 2006
Race: Great Wall of China Marathon
Time: 7:28:45
Note: I stopped and took over 100 photos during the race

MARATHON (STATE)	YEARS	YRS
Ft Worth's Cowtown (TX)	1982, 83, 85–91, 93–96, 99, 2000, 03, 04	17
Denton's NTSU (TX)	1982, 83	2
Wills Point's Day Break (TX)	1983	1
Dallas White Rock (TX)	1983–90, 92, 93, 95, 96, 98–00, 2003, 05–07	19
San Antonio (TX)	1998, 99, 2003	3
Dallas Trails (TX)	1993, 99–01, 2003, 04	6
Houston (TX)	2000, 01, 03	3
Austin (TX)	2000, 01	2
Walk of Fame (TX)	2000	1
Chicago LaSalle (IL)	2000	1
New Orleans Mardi Gras (LA)	2001	1
Nashville's Country Music (TN)	2001	1
Pacific Shoreline (CA)	2004	1

Spirit of Saint Louis (MO)	2004, 06	2
Race of Champions (MA)	2004	1
Tailwind Marathon (Denmark)	2004	1
Tupelo Marathon (MS)	2004	1
Oklahoma Marathon (Tulsa)	2004	1
Orange County Marathon (CA)	2004	1
Las Vegas Marathon (NV)	2005	1
Mercedes/Birmingham (AL)	2005	1
Little Rock (AR)	2005	1
Eisenhower (KS)	2005	1
Flying Pig (Cincinnati, OH)	2005	1
Keybank Vermont (VT)	2005	1
Gold Coast Airport (Australia)	2005	1
Iowa Trails 50K	2005	1
Lewis & Clark (MO)	2005	1
Hartford United Tech (CT)	2005	1
Myrtle Beach (SC)	2006	1
National (DC)	2006	1
New Jersey	2006	1
Great Wall of China	2006	1
New Mexico	2006	1
New Hampshire	2006	1
Tri-Cities (WA)	2006	1
Last Marathon (Antarctica)	2007	1
Fin Del Mundo (Argentina)	2007	1
ING Georgia (ATL)	2007	1
Salt Lake City (UT)	2007	1
Rite-Aid Cleveland	2007	1
Safaricom Lewa (Kenya)	2007	1
Heart of America (MO)	2007	1
Wineglass (NY)	2007	1
Philadelphia (PA)	2007	1

TOTAL MARATHONS　　　　　**91**

Running Shoes Are Cheaper Than Insulin

Selected Articles About Tony Reed

- February 2008 – "Human Race: Equal Footing," *Runners World.*
- November, 2007 – "The Last Word," *The Journal of Accountancy.*
- August, 2007 – "First Black Runner Finishes Marathon on all Seven Continents," *Runner Triathlete News.*
- July 17, 2007 – "Tony Reed Becomes First Black Runner To Finish Seven Marathons On Seven Continents," *Runners World.*
- July 17, 2007 – "Tony Reed: How I Became the First Black Runner to Complete Marathons on All Seven Continents," *Runners World.*
- May 18, 2007 – "Cleveland Marathon: A Foot Soldier for Blacks' Good Health," *The Plain Dealer* (Cleveland, OH).
- May/June, 2007 – "The Antarctica Marathon – The Marathon Texans Loved to Hate," *Inside Texas Running.*
- March 16, 2007 – "Some Cold Feet, But No Weak Knees – Antarctica Marathon," *The Dallas Morning News.*
- First Quarter, 2007 – "A Success Story – The Running Man," *Texins Magazine.*
- Fall, 2006 – "Great Wall Delivers a Great Adventure," *Travel News For Runners.*
- Sep/Oct, 2005 - NBMA to Gather at Lewis & Clark Marathon," *Missouri Runner and Triathlete.*
- February 28, 2005 – "A Brief Chat with Tony Reed," Runners World.
- January 30, 2005 – "Runners Keep Sport in Step with Times," The Ft. Worth (TX) *Star-Telegram.*
- April 25 and 26, 2005 – "Promoting Healthier Lives & Related Editorial," *The Cincinnati Enquirer.*

- March 5, 2004 – "Diabetes Hasn't Caught Up To Local Marathoner," *The Dallas Morning News*.
- March 3, 2004 – "50 Was Nifty for Dallas Marathoner," *The Ft. Worth Star-Telegram*.
- March, 2004 - featured as "*CPA and Former Wyman Camper and Counselor*" in Cornerstone for Kids campaign in support of Wyman and Camp Coca-Cola.
- Summer, 2003 - "Management Consultant Spends Free Time Running Marathons" *Webster (University) World*.
- March 28, 2003 – "Marathoner Reaches Goal Before 50," *The Dallas Morning News* Sports Section.
- July 28, 2002 – "IT Success Story," *Dallas Morning News*.
- November 19, 1999 – "TemporaryCIO.com review," *Dallas Business News* High-Tech Section.
- December, 1985 – "A Tale of Two Athletes," *News at 11K*.